T0196729

<u>Sadik Aboagye</u> offers an impressionistic view of rural life in Ghana with its concomitant challenges. For some of us, it is a reminder of the good old days in the village where basic amenities like good school, electricity, pipe-borne water, clinics, and others were virtually nonexistent, and still, life was normal and joyful. The book equally serves as a useful resource for all those who never tasted rural life but grew up in the cities of Ghana, Africa, and other countries.

The author experienced a myriad of problems and challenges with school, finances, fatal accidents, diseases, a snake bite, frustration, and perilous times on the deep-blue sea (Atlantic Ocean) aboard a ship from Nigeria to Ghana on two separate occasions, as well as many heart-breaking events in his life. Yet, the finger of God supported and protected him and his family in their journey of life.

The other side of the book is to encourage others to use and maximize available natural and human resources to propel themselves and society to greater heights. This is exemplified by the life of the author and his family in the two worlds of Ghana and the United States of America.

I am deeply honored to write these few lines about this timely and needed informative book.

Dr. Gabriel Amoateng-Boahen
Author and Professional Staff Chaplain
University of Chicago Medical Center

LIVING IN
TWO WORLDS

A Memoir

SADIK ABOAGYE

LIVING IN TWO WORLDS
A MEMOIR

iUniverse books may be ordered through booksellers or by contacting:

iUniverse
1663 Liberty Drive
Bloomington, IN 47403
www.iuniverse.com
1-800-Authors (1-800-288-4677)

ISBN: 978-1-4917-7959-0 (sc)
ISBN: 978-1-4917-7958-3 (e)

Library of Congress Control Number: 2015917464

Print information available on the last page.

iUniverse rev. date: 10/23/2015

This humble preparation is dedicated to my father, the late Sadik Kwadwo Bosompem, and mother, the late Sera Adwoa Fowaa, whose vision and courage enabled me to have a secondary school education in spite of their poverty.

*Success is to be measured not so much by the position
one has reached in life as by the obstacles which
he has overcome while trying to succeed.*
—Booker T. Washington

All great achievements require time.
—Maya Angelou

Surround yourself with only people who are going to lift you higher.
—Oprah Winfrey

Never be limited by other people's limited imaginations.
—Dr. Mae Jamison

*Try not to become a person of success, but
rather try to become a person of value.*
—Albert Einstein

Success is walking from failure to failure with no loss of enthusiasm.
—Winston Churchill

*I can accept failure, everyone fails at something,
but I cannot accept not trying.*
—Michael Jordan

*There are two types of people who will tell you that you
cannot make a difference in this world: Those who are
afraid to try and those who are afraid you will succeed.*
—Ray Goforth

Develop success from failures. Discouragement and
failure are the two surest stepping stones to success.
—Dale Carnegie

Each person must live their life as a model for others.
—Rosa Parks

We can't help everyone, but everyone can help someone.
—Ronald Reagan

You're not obligated to win. You're obligated to
keep trying to do your best every day.
—Marian Wright Edelman

Leadership and Learning are indispensable to each other.
—John F. Kennedy

Some see a hopeless end, while others see an endless hope.
—anonymous

It's not the years in your life that count, it's the life in your years.
—Abraham Lincoln

Good things come to people who wait, but better
things come to those who go out and get them.
—anonymous

As we express our gratitude, we must never forget that the
highest appreciation is not to utter words, but to live by them.
——John F. Kennedy

A successful man is one who can lay a firm foundation
with the bricks others have thrown at him.
—David Brinkley

Success does not consist in never making mistakes but
in never making the same one a second time.
—George Bernard Shaw

All our dreams can come true if we have
the courage to pursue them.
—Walt Disney

CONTENTS

————◆————

FOREWORD

———◆———

Mr. Sadik Bosompem Aboagye has chosen the title *Living in Two Worlds* for his memoir. When one has completed reading the work, one can understand why he settled on this title.

In the modern Ghanaian society, it is possible to come across people who might be rightly described as privileged. From childhood to adulthood, from birth to maturity, they have hardly known want. Living in the city with their parents, they have had such amenities as clean drinking water running from the tap instead of drinking water collected from guinea worm–infested streams.

Not for them the perils of the pit latrine into which one can fall easily but the modern water closet. Not for them the drudgery of farmwork with the perils of venomous snakes lurking in the undergrowth or the inconvenience of rain pouring down and soaking one's skin as one carries a heavy load of foodstuffs back home.

To the rural boy, even today, a telephone and electricity may be unheard-of luxuries. Where the community is a farming community, there may be plenty of food. However, in most cases, quality is sacrificed for quantity. Stunted growth brought about by poor nutrition is common. When the boy or girl growing up in a rural area has no model to look up to, it takes a great deal of courage and determination to get anywhere.

What Mr. Aboagye tells us in his memoir is a simple but impressive story of a struggle to overcome the nearly insurmountable difficulties of a boy without privileges growing up in a deprived rural area.

I taught Mr. Aboagye at T.I. AMASS. When I became the headmaster of the school in 1990, Mr. Aboagye was already there as a teacher. He was also the secretary of the Parent-Teacher Association (PTA). During the eight years that I was the headmaster, from 1990 to 1998, I found Mr. Aboagye hardworking, humble, respectful, and totally unassuming. He always had a ready smile that was genuine. To teach his students very well, he prepared good teaching aids in the form of pamphlets at a time when there were no textbooks on Islamic religious knowledge, which was the subject he taught.

What this simple and unsophisticated rural boy goes through before he finally makes it to the United States of America is a story everyone should know and learn from. It shows that a person need not be born in a privileged home before he can make good use of his God-given talents in order to transform his life from one of hopelessness to one of hope for a better life.

Mr. Aboagye had a relatively large family. Even then, though no longer young, he had the determination to pursue further studies at the University of Ghana–Legon and the University of Winneba in Ghana.

With his rural background, many would have been content with passing the Middle School Leaving Certificate Examination. I am happy to note that his determination and perseverance paid off academically when he earned not only a diploma but also a degree.

In this country, we say, "Travel and see." Mr. Aboagye's stay in the United States clearly broadens his mind greatly, if it does nothing else.

By the grace of God and through his own exertions, Mr. Aboagye has clearly lifted himself from the pit of despondency to the height of achievement.

I.K. Gyasi
Former Headmaster
T.I. Ahmadiyya Secondary School
Kumasi

PREFACE

The objective of this memoir is an attempt to tell my life story in a chronological document for the benefit of my children and descendants, all in the United States, with some of them born here in Chicago. It is my belief that some will inquire about the genealogy of the family in the future, and this will serve as a perfect source of information. It will inform them about when, how, and from where their ancestors migrated to the United States. It also serves as history to the children and the generations yet to come about the landscape and educational and social developments of my village, Anyanso, in the Bosome/Freho District of the Ashanti Region of Ghana, West Africa.

About six and half decades ago, my village had a lot of forestland that served as a sanctuary for birds and other creatures. The streams and rivers were flowing in abundance, thus giving the land the needed fertility. Currently, all the swampy lands have dried up because of the abuse of the land, and this has negatively affected the rivers and streams in the area, which have also dried up. Once a busy cocoa-growing area that made the inhabitants relatively richer by their standards, the land has now become predominantly a food crop–growing area and has adversely affected the incomes of the inhabitants.

With population growth and its attendant expansion of the village, the amount of land owned by individuals for farming has reduced. The result is inadequate food production to feed the ever-growing population. This has compelled the youth to move to the cities to find alternative work, learn some trade, or attend postprimary institutions.

There is the need for the limited land to be judiciously used and protected. This can be done through reforestation and avoiding bushfires caused by hunters and other land users.

I was born and bred in a rural setting, having lived there throughout my teenage years, and I started my teaching career at the same village of Anyanso. In my village, basic social, educational, health care, and other related facilities were lacking. Some teachers, especially those who lived in the towns and cities, refused postings to my village as a result of the lack of such facilities. I later moved from Anyanso to another town, Asokore in the Sekyere District of Ashanti Region. Thereafter, I pursued a higher education at the University of Ghana–Legon. This new upgrade in my life enabled me to live in the city of Kumasi, where necessary facilities were available. When I became settled in Kumasi as a secondary school teacher, I moved my family from the village to live with me in the city.

From 1981 through 1997, I was predominantly in Kumasi with the exception of a few years as a sojourner in Nigeria and two years at the University of Winneba. In 1997 at Winneba, I entered the American Diversity Visa Lottery, and by the grace of God, I was one of the lucky beneficiaries. This afforded me the opportunity to travel to the United States in 1999, and I have lived in the city of Chicago ever since. According to Lisa Nichols in her book *You Can Overcome Every Obstacle … No Matter What*, "In order for me to tell you how good my life is now, I have to tell you how much of a mess it was before. It's the only way you could adequately understand the miracle of my journey."

My life has been full of adventures, though there may be some other people who might have gone through similar or worse experiences than mine. To such people, this piece might be reminiscent of their pasts. There may be others who might view this write-up as a mere concoction of stories or a figment of my imagination. I was among thousands of Ghanaians expelled from Nigeria, a neighboring country, on two separate occasions in 1983 and 1985 because I had no resident permit. I had therefore resolved never to travel to any other country unless I had the required documents to make my stay trouble-free. My journey to America, I believed, answered my resolution. According to Nichols, "You are the architect of your own life. You hold the key to your own success or failure."

Immigration has some advantages, but sometimes it can be disadvantageous to some people, especially when the immigrant does not possess a valid resident permit. The notion of deportation anytime keeps haunting that individual. Dr. Kofi Teye, a researcher at the center of migration studies, University of Ghana–Legon, agrees that "there are positive aspects of migration but most often society turns to ignore that and concentrate only on negatives. He said apart from improving their socio-economic well-being, most migrants are better off than when they were in their towns of origin." Patience Azaglo Gbeze of Ghana News Agency said, "It is not everything about migration that is negative and if people get to know the success story of some migrants they would change their views on the issue" (a publication of the *Ghanaian Chronicle Newspaper*, September 16, 2014).

It is my belief that those who have the opportunity to read this book will gain some experience and will be able to compare and contrast a village life and a city life in Ghana, as well as in the United States, and make judicious conclusions for themselves. However, the title of the book is not necessarily meant to compare and contrast the developed and developing nations. Such a comparison will amount to an act of injustice. Rather, the book is meant to let readers from one side of the globe have an insight into the other side for a better understanding of the other's anthropology, sociology, economy, and overall behavioral patterns for now and posterity.

Sadik Bosompem Aboagye Sr.
Chicago, Illinois
United States of America

ACKNOWLEDGMENTS

This publication is dedicated to my late father Sadik Kwadwo Bosompem and late mother Serah Adwoa Fowaa, whose vision and toil enabled me to have a secondary school education at the expense of their pleasure. My heartfelt gratitude goes to my brothers and sisters whose assistance to my parents helped me in my secondary school education. Also worthy of thanks are my aunts, the late Amma Donkor (Amma Birago) and the late Amma Konadu, who helped my father during my secondary education after the death of my mother.

I should also like to express my sincere appreciation to the late Mr. Yusuf K. Effah, the former headmaster of T.I. Ahmadiyya Secondary School (also known as T.I. AMASS) in Kumasi, for unearthing my potential while I was working with him. I must also show gratitude to Mr. I.K. Gyasi, former headmaster, and Mrs. E.B. Ntiforo, former assistant headmaster, both of whom were my former English teachers at T.I. AMASS for their counseling and inspiration during my teaching years at T.I. AMASS between 1981 and 1997.

Furthermore, my family and I owe a debt gratitude to Nana Akwasi Addae, ex-Asantefuohene (chief) of Chicago, and his wife, Obaapanin Abena Addae; Mr. Fred Seng of Northwest Ford and

Sterling Truck Center in Chicago, Nana's white American friend; and Mr. Kwadwo Antwi, alias Bob, for their moral, material, and financial assistance, which made our migration to America possible.

Also worthy of my thankfulness are my friends the Messrs. Abdullah Mahmud Sam, Rockson William Fosu, Alhaj Othman Yahya, Nana Kwame Adarkwah, and Rockson Harun Agyare, as well as my cousins, Hon. Kwadwo Kyei-Frimpong and James Asare, for their support and assistance in cash and kind during my struggles in life.

Personalities like Mr. John Osei Asamoah, alias Nana Yaw Asamoah, and Mr. Seth K. Owusu, alias Nana Yaw Sarfo, deserve my family's gratitude for their invaluable assistance with the immigration of my children whom I left behind in Ghana. Nana Akwasi Appiah, ex-Asantefuohene of Chicago, and Nana Andy Yaw Aninagyei cannot be left out in this acknowledgment for their assistance in our initial job acquisition in Chicago.

I must express my profound gratitude to John Henry Assabill, the former president of the Ghana National Council, through whom I had the opportunity to serve the Ghanaian community in the Ghana National Council of Metropolitan Chicago. The Asanteman Association of Chicago and Midwest also deserve my appreciation, as my membership of such a big family enhanced my personal and social well-being in Chicago. Members of the Ghana National Council of Metropolitan Chicago, both past and present, equally deserve my appreciation for a very cordial coexistence and friendship.

I should express my heartfelt appreciation to Dr. Gabriel Amoateng Boahen, whom I consulted on numerous occasions—in fact, at every stage of this publication. I am equally grateful to Dr. Alie Kabba for reading through this piece and offering very useful suggestions for this accomplishment.

I cannot end my acknowledgment without mentioning my dear wife, Mariam Tenewah Aboagye, for her patience, endurance, and understanding during the periods of difficulties, anguish, and frustration in my life. All my children equally deserve my gratitude for their support of all kinds in my life.

The plight of rural children forever remains my utmost concern.

Above all, my greatest gratitude goes to Almighty God whose grace and guidance throughout my life helped me to get out of the vicious cycle of poverty that engulfed my parents.

Sadik Bosompem Aboagye Sr.
Chicago, Illinois
United States of America

ABSTRACT

The purpose of this publication is to leave a legacy for my children and grandchildren, all of whom live in the United States, as well as those yet unborn who might be interested in searching for their ancestry in the future. The book details how, when, and from where the family migrated from a rural community of Anyanso in the Ashanti Region of Ghana, West Africa, to Chicago, Illinois, the United States.

It also enlightens the reader that success can be achieved through determination, hard work, perseverance, and focus as exemplified by the author's life experiences from childhood through adult life. He was the child of poor farmers in a village who grew up with series of challenges, including farmwork with the attendant wounds from cutlass cuts and thorns, snake bites, school financial constraints, diseases, motor accidents, deportations, uncertainties, and frustrations. Yet, with God's guidance, he eventually made it to the United States.

This book, among others, serves as a resource for readers in different parts of the world to have an insight into different cultures of other parts of the world. It can be a very useful material for students and prospective travelers, especially from the developing countries who want to seek greener pastures elsewhere.

INTRODUCTION

I was born to poor farmers in a rural community of Anyanso in the Ashanti Region of Ghana to the late Sadik Kwadwo Bosompem and the late Sera Adwoa Fowaa. My father and mother died when I was in secondary school, about three years apart. My mother died on May 4, 1966, and my father died on November 17, 1969. In addition to the deaths of my parents, I experienced some challenges and obstacles in both my childhood and adult life.

I grew up in an extended family home with my parents, siblings, uncles, and their families. I started my primary school education at Anyanso Methodist Primary School at the age of six. My village was devoid of social amenities like good school, good drinking water, medical facilities, electricity, housing, and good sanitation when compared to the urban areas where these social amenities were available. Like other children of rural communities, my daily routine was to bathe and fetch water from the river in the mornings before going to school. On weekends, after fetching water from the river, I had to accompany my parents to the farm. As a child, I had to carry the water that would be used in preparing our meals and for drinking. When the water was gone before the end of the day's work, I had to fetch some

1

from a nearby river or stream with either my siblings or children of other nearby farmers.

Our school had inadequate enrollment, so some classes were combined with a single teacher. When I was in fourth grade, our class was combined with fourth, fifth, and sixth grades. On completion of sixth grade I had to transfer to Asiwa Presbyterian Middle School, because there was no middle school in my village. Asiwa is about six miles from Anyanso. Some of us who did not have relatives in the towns with middle schools were compelled to walk to Asiwa for our middle school education. We made the six-mile walk each way on the days we attended school. The journey to Asiwa was a footpath halfway and dusty or feeder road from Anyinase, the next village, to Asiwa.

Walking in weedy footpaths with gullies in some places was very dreadful. Sometimes we would come across a snake chasing its prey, and we would either retreat or attempt to kill it. Logs were used as bridges over the streams. During the rainy seasons when the streams became flooded, we had to return home. When I was in middle form four, I had to stay with my paternal uncle during the weekdays so I could attend the night classes usually organized by the class teacher for the examination class. I went to Anyanso on the weekends. Asiwa served as the education center in the neighboring communities; as such, there were some secondary school students in that town. Some of those students visited our school when they were on vacation.

I took the Common Entrance Examination when I was in middle form four, even though I knew my parents could not afford the school fees. However, I finished middle school and passed the Middle School Leaving Certificate Examination. With no expectation of a secondary school education, my father told me one day that we would go to Kumasi the following week. Kumasi is the second largest city in Ghana and the capital of

Ashanti Region. To my utter surprise, my father, through his friend who was a circuit missionary of the Ahmadiyya Mission, sought admission for me at the Ahmadiyya Secondary School. A new chapter had opened in my life.

When school reopened on September 28, 1964, my father accompanied me to the T.I. AMASS. His missionary friend, Abdul Wahid, led me through the admission procedure. A day before the reopening, my father and I visited my aunt Madam Abena Asubonteng, with whom I would stay for my secondary school education, because my father could not afford the boarding fees.

I started school in earnest but faced so many challenges in the course of my studies. The fact that I was a day student walking for about two miles to and from school each day and had a myriad of household chores to complete weighed heavily on my studies. We were five people in a single room, all females except me. I had to wake up early in the morning to stand in line for water from the standing taps outside our house for the morning use. The whole household had just one toilet and one bath, so in the morning, people had to keep waiting to use either of the two facilities. Thereafter, I would have to prepare to make the two-mile walk to school. Upon returning from school, I had other work to do before the night.

There were a lot of inmates in that compound house, and noisemaking was very rampant. No part of the building was conducive to studies. Sometimes I had to walk back to school in order to study. The cumulative effect of the aforementioned factors caused deterioration in my academic performance.

Upon repeated complaints to my father, he sent me to the boarding house during my third year in school. Though this was a big relief, the problem of paying the school fees cropped up. I could never pay my school fees in full. I had to make negotiated payments every term till I completed secondary school. During every school break, I had to go back to my village to assist my parents in the farming activities. One day as I was returning from the farm, I experienced a snake bite and had to undergo traditional treatment.

I completed my secondary school education in June 1970, but unfortunately, when the results were released in early September, some of the subjects were canceled nationwide due to leakage of some of the subjects. The affected students had to retake those subjects in November that same year. I then decided to apply for a teaching position as uncertificated teacher in the Bekwai District Education office. I was posted to a village called Nsuta.

While teaching, I had my eyes on a teacher-training college for a postsecondary teacher's certificate to become a professional teacher. I gained admission to the Bagabaga Teacher Training College on October 10, 1971. I returned to my village for the Christmas break. On Tuesday, December 28, 1971, I fractured my left leg while playing soccer with friends. This incident compelled me to stay home for more than three months while I received painful traditional treatment. I completed the two-year course on July 31, 1973. I started teaching in my village, Anyanso, on September 18, 1973.

I spent four years teaching in my village before transferring to another town, Asokore, in the Sekyere District. In January 1976 I married my wife, Mariam Tenewaa Aboagye. In December 1976 we had our first child, Hanna Boampomaa Aboagye. Barely three months after giving birth, my wife suffered from a prolonged malaria sickness that lasted for more than three months. This put me in a state of uneasiness and frustration. By God's grace, she recovered, and the baby was not harmed in anyway.

In Anyanso, I was the secretary to the Town Development Committee. I also combined farming with teaching as a second job. I spent two years at Asokore Ahmadiyya Middle School and then proceeded to complete a two-year diploma course in the study of Religions and Philosophy at the University of Ghana–Accra, the national capital of Ghana. I started the course on September 10, 1979, and graduated on June 27, 1981. I offered my one-year mandatory national service assignment at AMASS and thereafter traveled to Nigeria on September 15, 1982, with the hope of a better life, but that hope vanished when those of us without resident permits were deported to our various countries on January 17, 1983. I made a second attempt to Nigeria on September 10, 1983, but again, we were deported in May 1985. In both instances, I returned to Ghana on a ship provided by the government of Ghana.

Upon my return to Ghana in May 1985, I reapplied to the Ghana Education Service for reappointment. The headmaster, the late Y.K. Effah, was very instrumental to get me posted to teach at AMASS in September 1985. While there, I was the secretary of the Parent-Teacher Association from 1985 till I left the school in 1997 for further studies at the University of Winneba. It was at Winneba that I won the American Diversity Visa Lottery that enabled me, my wife, and our children to travel to the United States in 1999, in spite of the uncertainties and very demanding process of the visa acquisition.

When we eventually obtained our visas, we left the shores of Ghana on Tuesday, August 24, 1999. We experienced a flight delay and finally arrived in New York on Thursday, August 26, 1999. We boarded the Greyhound bus from New York City to Chicago and arrived at about one o'clock on the morning of Friday, August 27, 1999.

Nana Akwasi Addae assisted us in obtaining our Social Security numbers and the State Identity cards that would enable us to look for jobs. I started work at a parking garage as a cashier, then at O'Hare International Airport as a passenger service agent, and later a second job as a substitute teacher with the Chicago Public Schools. Currently, I am Public Chauffeur at the city of Chicago under the Department of Business Affairs and Consumer Protection (BACP).

I am actively involved in the Ghanaian community activities in Chicago and am the current executive secretary of the Ghana National Council of Metropolitan Chicago, the umbrella organization of all the Ghanaian associations in Chicago. I also served in various executive positions in the previous administration of the council. I am also the recording secretary to the Asanteman Association of Chicago and Midwest, one of the affiliate organizations of the Ghana National Council.

CHAPTER 1

BACKGROUND

Maternal Ancestry

My mother, Madam Serah Adwoa Fowaa, was born around 1911 in Tebeso in the Bosome Freho District of the Ashanti Region of Ghana. My maternal grandparents were Opanin Yaw Amoah and Adwoa Kordie. Some years after my mother was born, my grandmother left Tebeso to settle at Anyanso about ten miles away. My mother had one maternal half brother named Yaw Kyei and three maternal half sisters, Amma Donkor (Birago), Amma Konadu, and Amma Anane (Boampomaa).

Amma Donkor married Opanin Kwaku Kyei of Nsuaem, where she settled with her family. She was blessed with four children, Elizabeth Kyei Frema, Mary Kyei Boatemaa, Hon. Kwadwo Kyei Frimpong (a member of parliament (MP) in Ghana), and Charles Kyei Baffour, in that order. At the time of writing this piece, only Kwadwo Kyei Frimpong is alive.

Madam Amma Konadu married Opanin Kwasi Amoako of Anwhiaso, where she and her descendants lived. She had eight children: Yaa Kete, Akosua Krah, Charles Amoako, Akua

Abonne, William Amoako, Isaac Amoako, Georgina Amoako, and Akua Badu. Only Yaa Kete has died as of now.

My mother also had some paternal half siblings, including, but not limited to, Kofi Nyame, Adwoa Nyame, Abena Asubonteng, and Akua Simune, who all lived in Tebeso in the same district.

My mother gave birth to eleven children, three of whom died at birth according to my late mother. The names of the survivors in birth order were: Akosua Buroni, Akosua Amina, Akosua Madina, Akosua Fatima, Hakeem Adjei-Twum (Kwasi Agyei), Yaa Abrafi, Adjei Zakariya (Yaw Kordie), and myself. At the time of this writing, Fatima, Hakeem, and I are living.

My mother's other sister, Amma Anane, gave birth to two daughters, Adwoa Birago and Yaa Kordie, who died at an early age. Adwoa Birago is still alive. My mother, Adwoa Fowaa; her sister Amma Anane; and their brother Yaw Kyei remained at Anyanso. Prior to their marriage, my father had married one Amma Oyie and had a son named Yaw Boadi. My mother had also married one Opanin Kwaku Agyei and had one daughter, Akosua Buroni.

I stayed with my parents at the family house, Aborosanase, with my late uncles, Yaw Kyei, D.K. Forson (Kwabena Anane), and Kwadwo Krah, as well as the wives of Forson and Kwadwo Krah and their children.

As the youngest boy living with my uncles, I was the errand person to give information to other relatives in the nearby villages of Nsuaem, Tebeso, Nsutem, Anhwiaso, Amomorso, Freso, and sometimes Saponso. All these journeys were made on foot, the distance ranging between five and twenty miles. The house was called Aborosanase because it was the only two-story building at Anyanso and the surrounding villages at the time. We had three maternal grandfathers, Afarwua, Kwaning, and Tuffour, who was the youngest.

The home was built around 1935 by one of our maternal grandfathers, Kwadwo Tuffour, and it remained as such till about 2003 when another was built by Nana Akwasi Addae (ex-Asantefuohene of Chicago) and his brother Kwadwo Antwi (Bob). Upon my grandfather's death, Uncle Yaw Kyei succeeded him. In 1970 when Uncle Yaw Kyei died, Uncle Kwaku Tawiah became the lineage head. Currently, my cousin Kwadwo Kyei Frimpong is the lineage head elected in 2010 upon the demise of Kwaku Tawiah. Hon. Kwadwo Kyei Frimpong is also a member of parliament for Bosome-Freho constituency.

Any time the Catholic priests, whites by then, visited their congregation in my village and the surrounding communities, they were hosted at our home because of the airy nature upstairs. The top floor consisted of two bedrooms and a big living room, so the priests put up their tents in the living room. Thus the inmates and the descendants are called Aborosanasefuo at Anyanso.

Paternal Ancestry

My father, the late Sadik Kwadwo Bosompem alias Srekye (corrupted name for Sadik), was born about 1903 in the village of Pipiiso near Obuasi in the Adansi South District of the Ashanti Region of Ghana. He later moved with his brother Ebenezer Kwaku Asare to settle in Asiwa in the Bosome-Freho District of the Ashanti Region. As a child, I once accompanied my father, mother, and sister Fatima to my father's village of Pipiiso, a distance of more than fifteen miles on a footpath through farmlands. After some distance, my father would carry me on his shoulders for some time, especially where the path was waterlogged and muddy.

My father first married Amma Oyie, but that marriage did not last long. The story goes that my father was a heavy drunkard, and one day in his drunken mood, he went to the house of his in-laws and insulted them over an issue with his wife. The family became annoyed and thereafter dissolved the marriage. Upon realizing his mistake and the dissolution of his marriage, my father instantly converted to Islam Ahmadiyya and became a staunch member of the Ahmadiyya Muslim community. In addition to his first two marriages, my father married Madam Sakina from Adansi Domeabra near Obuasi in the Ashanti Region and had two children with her, Ibrahim Sadik and Khadija. This marriage also lasted for a few years, which I hardly observed, as I was then a child. I was the eleventh son of my mother and the tenth of my father.

History has it that for some time my father was a well-to-do person by the village's standard, owning a petty shop and a chain of cocoa farms at Asiwa where he had settled earlier. He later lost all his wealth due to prolonged litigation with his uncle over a vehicle they purchased. His cocoa farms were auctioned to defray the debt he incurred in his litigation. One of his lenders happened to be Opanin Kwaku Bosie of Anyanso, whose nephew, Opanin Kofi Afoakwa (Kofi Salifu), was the husband of one of my sisters. Opanin Kwaku Bosie was kind enough to hire my father take care of the cocoa farms. My father therefore became the caretaker of his own cocoa farms. As a result of my father's litigation, my two elder brothers, Emmanuel Yaw Boadi (who was one of the pioneers of T.I. AMASS) and Hakeem Agyei-Twum (who was also at the Normal Technical School at Koforidua), had to drop out of school for lack of money. This adversely affected my two older brothers in their future lives. In spite of all these challenges, having lost his petty shop and cocoa farms, my father was determined to make life meaningful with his farming activities, including growing food crops and legumes, being a caretaker of his lost cocoa farms, working as a tailor, and weaving metal fishing traps.

I was born in September 1950 to the late Sadik Kwadwo Bosompem, popularly called Kramo Srekye (corrupted form of

Sadik), an Ahmadi convert, and the late Madam Sera Adwoa Fowaa in Anyanso. Anyanso is situated in the newly created Bosome-Freho District of Ashanti, a tropical rainforest region of Ghana. The district was carved out of the Amansie East District and was inaugurated by former President John Agyekum Kufuor on February 29, 2008, in Asiwa, the district capital.

Primary Education

I attended the Anyanso Methodist Primary School at the age of six or thereabout. The teacher who inspired me most during my primary school days was the late Issah Agyeman, who happened to teach me in third grade. Incidentally, I taught three of his children at Ahmadiyya Secondary School in Kumasi later in life. He taught us Islamic religious knowledge in addition to his normal academic subjects. He ensured that the Muslim children attended the mosque, especially for Friday afternoon prayers (*Jumah Salat*), night prayers, and morning prayers. He also taught us some Koranic chapters (*Surah*) for prayers.

Even though I was a bright student and the first in the class at the time of final examinations, there were occasions when I failed to attend school for no obvious reasons. On one such occasion, a detachment of the big boys in my class came home to "arrest" me at the command of my class teacher. On another occasion when I stayed away from school, I knew very well that my classmates would come to our houses to arrest me, so I joined my playmates and hid in an orange grove. When we saw the search group, we all bolted, and I ran to my parents' farm where they least expected to find me.

When I was in fourth grade, we shared the same classroom with students in fifth and sixth grades due to inadequate enrollment. We had one teacher named Mr. Mensah who was an expert in caning. On Friday mornings we had music lessons, and he made sure that students were disciplined for failing to sing to the proper tune. Because of his strictness and caning, some kids dropped out of school, especially the dull students who could not withstand his caning. Every morning he conducted a twenty-question quiz, and the number of mistakes you made was the number of strokes of the cane you received.

The following year I was promoted from fourth grade to sixth grade, skipping fifth grade to augment the enrolment to eight, even though I was in the same combined class. We had new teachers, Mr. Adu, who was also the new head teacher, and Mr. Addo. These two teachers performed great work in the school. I was made the assistant school prefect for that year and was given the responsibility of writing the names of students who stayed on the streets at night instead of remaining indoors to study from Monday to Friday. The defaulters were disciplined by corporal punishment in the form of caning at the next morning's assembly.

One Saturday night, as we were sitting in front of a petty shop, some grown-up boys were singing some profane songs. Mr. Adu happened to come to the store to buy something and heard the song. The next Monday morning, those of us spotted by Mr. Adu were called to the front at assembly and given twelve strokes of the cane. Our offense was that we were listening to profane songs at a time we were supposed to be at home learning.

My best friend at the primary school was Kwame Mensah, the son of the owner of a petty shop in my village. Sometimes it gave me the opportunity to taste some palatable stew at lunch during the break from the morning school session. What interested me most during my primary school days was the occasion of Our Day when we gathered in our classrooms to enjoy a feast on the last day of school. Each student would bring the best meal he or she could afford. Thereafter, the bell would be rung for assembly for the final results to be released and read to the whole gathering. Usually the head teacher would read the results from first through sixth grades. It was a happy moment for the bright students but a sad day for the dull ones. We would be singing and teasing our friends who did not perform well, which often led to fights among some students.

As with some rural schools even today, students were asked to fetch water and firewood for our teachers, especially after the morning session. At times we had to miss classes to fetch water, sand, or gravel for people in the community in order to raise money for some essential items like football, jerseys, end-of-the-year parties, or first-aid medications for the school. Sometimes we would be required to bring a certain number of cups of palm nuts or a bunch of brooms or baskets to school on Monday as part of the fund-raising efforts.

In my childhood days, my happiest moments were during Christmas celebrations and the two *Eid* festivals, *Eidul Adzha* (festival of sacrifice) and *Eidul Fitr* (festival after the fasting month). These are the two yearly Muslim festivals. I enjoyed these times so much, because these were the occasions when I might receive new clothes and a pair of sandals or canvas shoes. Moreover, these were the periods when we could have out-of-the-ordinary meals, that is yam with beans and sardines or corned-beef stew with eggs in the mornings and chicken and groundnut soup in the evenings.

As a child, I liked the month of Ramadan (the Muslim month of fasting), because I knew that my breakfast was assured. My mother used to reserve some of the meals that she prepared for my father and my elder brethren at dawn for us. The only meals known to me and other rural children were *Ampesi* (cooked yam, plantain, and cocoyam) in the mornings and *fufu* (a local meal) in the evenings. When I grew up a little and was able to pound *fufu*, I was called to partake in the pounding and also took part in the fasting. At times it was very unpleasant to wake up at dawn, especially in the cold weather.

As there was no electricity in my village, moonlight days were very welcome, because we had a lot of time to play on the streets before going to bed very late in the night. Sometimes we would gather in one spot and listen to folktales (Ananse stories) from some of our elders. Occasionally, there would be a mobile cinema in the village in an open spot. The children would squat or sit on the dusty ground to watch the film, which was usually an educational program.

Not only did we lack electricity, but we also didn't have good and treated drinking water. We fetched water from the rivers and streams. Sometimes when it rained and the rivers became flooded, the water became very dirty as a result of the eroded materials that found their way into the rivers. In such cases, the water must be kept for some time for the sediment to settle. On the contrary, during the dry season when the streams and rivers were drastically lower, we had to clear off some of the fallen leaves on the surface before we could draw some water. The duty of children was usually to fetch water for the home, as well as going to the farm. The most painful aspect of it was if you fell on the way and the bucket of water poured off; then you had to return to the river or stream to fetch more. While we worked on the farm and there was water shortage, the children had to fetch more water, especially during the dry season when the temperatures were high, resulting in high demand for water. A place of convenience was the pit latrine, and when on the farm, one would have to defecate in a bush.

There was no middle school in my village, and the same was true in some of the surrounding villages; some of us had to continue our middle school education in Asiwa, which had the only middle school near to us. Those who had relatives in other towns with middle schools had to go and live with them for their middle school education. Asiwa was the education hub in the surrounding villages. It had well-established primary and middle schools at the time when the neighboring communities had no middle schools. Some of the secondary school students used to visit the middle school when they were on vacation, and we had some interactions with some of them.

CHAPTER 2

TEENAGE YEARS

Middle School Education

On Tuesday, September 12, 1960, I transferred from Anyanso Methodist Primary School to Asiwa Presbyterian Middle School. The first problem I encountered with the school administration was during the presentation of transfer certificates. When I received my transfer certificate from my former primary school head teacher, I crossed out my name on the certificate, which was listed as Abubakar Srekye, and wrote *Kwasi Aboagye* to conform to the person I was named after without my father's knowledge. When the head teacher, Mr. Francis Asiam Attuah, and his staff invited me to the office and queried me about the change, I stood naively before them, not knowing the seriousness of the offense. My father was invited to the school, and the head teacher demanded a fresh certificate. My father and I went back to my former head teacher, who willingly issued a new certificate to me.

Asiwa is about six miles from my village of Anyanso. It was a difficult task trekking six miles each way five days a week. However, some of us managed to undertake it with determination and perseverance for our four years of middle school education. Asiwa Presbyterian Middle School was a focal point of education, as it was the only middle school in the surrounding villages. Currently, Asiwa is the capital of the Bosome/Freho District, so it doesn't surprise me that it has one of the only rural secondary schools in the area to serve the community. Students from Anyanso, Anyinase, Freboye, Nsuaem, Danso, and Brofoyedru all trekked to Asiwa for their middle school education. This enabled the middle school to attract both bright and dull students from these villages; hence, competition was very keen in the various classes.

Every morning my mother made sure she prepared some food for me before I left for school at about seven o'clock, because my parents could not afford to give me pocket money for school each day. By the time I returned from bathing in the river, my food would be ready, and I would hurriedly eat. Sometimes, when my friends were already leaving for school, I had to carry the food and eat it during our walk.

The journey to school in Asiwa was along a footpath from Anyanso to Anyinase and then a feeder road from Anyinase to Asiwa, which was better for us. Rural communities used logs as bridges to cross the rivers and streams, which was scary especially, when the rivers overflowed. The most difficult times were during the rainy seasons. Whenever the streams and rivers became flooded and we could not cross, we had to return home. At times, we left home before the rain started and had no option but to continue the journey to school. We usually used plantain leaves as umbrellas, while our books were packed on our backs to keep them dry. We would reach school drenched, especially during the morning rains. The evening rains with their accompanying thunderstorms were dreadful. Walking barefooted on a muddy and weedy footpath with gullies was a challenging experience, but some of us endured it for four years.

When we were late for school, we were not spared punishment, so we used to hide in the bushes while everyone was at the assembly and then sneak to our classrooms. Sometimes we were driven out to do our assignments on our plots. On some occasions when our school had to play a football match against other schools, we left Asiwa after the game at about six thirty in the evening instead of the normal four o'clock. We walked home in the dark and arrived home very late. But if the game was played in another town, we ran away when we were dismissed to trek to that town if it was not on our way home. On some lucky days, we would get free transport in a wooden vehicle from Asiwa to Anyinase to shorten our walking distance and time. In spite of all these difficulties, we were cheerful friends, especially when we were returning from school amid teasing, quarreling, and fighting with the big boys bullying the little ones.

During the harvesting periods of such fruits as oranges, pawpaw, pineapples, and bananas, we enjoyed ourselves most, because on our way back from school, we ate a lot and pocketed the remaining fruit or hid them somewhere in the bush so we could take them to school the next day. Unfortunately, these wild fruits that we enjoyed in those days have vanished due to the abuse of the land. They were very predominant in the bush, as well as the outskirts of the village.

My best friends in middle school were Ayub Agyekum (now deceased), Abdullah Agyabeng, and Yaw Obeng (now a high school teacher in New York City), even though I was a year or more ahead of them in school. My niece Mariam Yaa Nimakowaa was also my classmate in the middle school, although she was living with her father in Anyinase. Sometimes, when we were returning from school, I would accompany her to her house, and if food was ready, I would enjoy some before continuing my journey to Anyanso. On Saturdays, I used to accompany my parents to the farm, and on Sundays, I accompanied my mother and older sisters to Asiwa market to sell some of her food products. Sundays were market days in Asiwa, so farmers from the surrounding villages brought foodstuffs they were offering for sale. Carrying foodstuffs for a distance of about six miles was a difficult task, but that was the lot of rural dwellers.

On our return from the marketplace, we would go to the river to wash our clothes in the afternoon. After the washing and waiting for the sun to dry our clothes, my playmates and I would go into the swampy forests to hunt for crabs, regardless of the risks of snake bites, thorns, and brambles. We would then sell what we found to get a few pennies for pocket money, although this was against my father's will. Sometimes we would return home very late in the afternoon to sell our products.

As children, we would be told to go to the bush to hunt for snails and mushrooms for the evening meals while our parents worked on the farm. In the course of hunting, we would sometimes come across a snake or a bunch of wasps and would run helter-skelter for our dear lives. That would not deter us from going to the bush the next time. Most of the time, we had to go to the farm barefoot, walking through swampy and weedy footpaths in tattered clothes.

We used to carry some foodstuffs to Asiwa to prepare lunch when the morning session was over. We usually gathered in groups in various houses owned by someone related to a friend to prepare lunch. My friends and I were preparing lunch in my paternal family's house. As a practice, we were supposed to fetch water to replenish what we used to cook our meals, but sometimes we forgot, and the next day we would receive insults and threats of being driven away from the house.

The practice of fetching water and firewood was not limited to the primary school alone. Sometimes we had to skip classes to fetch sand, gravel, and water for either our teachers or to raise money for the school. At other times, we had to fetch bamboo to either fence our school garden to keep away stray sheep and goats or to fence the school football field.

The head teacher of the school was Mr. Francis Asiam Attuah, a devout Presbyterian teacher who ensured that music periods were fully observed by all students. Any student found to be playing the fool would be severely disciplined. He was a very hardworking head teacher.

The teacher who inspired me most was Mr. Owusu-Antwi, our form three teacher. He was so dedicated to his work that he made sure our homework was always fully completed. He instituted what he termed the Big Six, which was what he called the six potential students in his class. He was so strict on the six of us that any mistakes in our work attracted the cane; be it mathematics, mental arithmetic, English comprehension, composition, construction, dictation, spelling, or vocabulary, which were each tracked in a separate exercise book.

The six of us were Opoku Jackson; Asantewaa Beatrice 1 and Asantewaa Beatrice 2 (the twin daughters of our head teacher); Alice Pinaman (the daughter of the head teacher of the primary school); Agyei Dominic; and me. At the end of the academic year, Opoku Jackson gained admission to Asankragua Secondary School with a full scholarship. He later graduated from the University of Ghana with a major in Economics. The rest of us, with the exception of Agyei Dominic, attended secondary schools after our form-four examination. Alice Pinaman later graduated from the University of Cape Coast, and the two Asantewaa girls attended the Nurses Training College and are nurses at the Agogo Presbyterian Hospital. I attended Ahmadiyya Secondary School in Kumasi, Bagabaga Teacher Training College in Tamale, University of Ghana, and then University College of Education at Winneba.

Agyei Dominic, who could not attend any secondary school, learned to become a tailor in Accra and later traveled abroad.

In middle form four, there were some bad boys who gave the teachers a lot of problems. Some of them were tapping palm wine, and when the head teacher discovered it, he accompanied them to the site to bring the pots and calabashes to the school. He called an instant assembly of all the students and brought the culprits with their pots in front of the whole school. They were given the appropriate caning punishment. With such behavior, coupled with inconsistent attendance at night studies by some of our mates, our head teacher did not take much interest in the night studies program he had organized for the final-year students.

During that period, our examination center for the Middle School Leaving Certificate was at Bekwai, the district capital, which was about seventy miles from Asiwa. We had to travel through Kumasi as there was no direct road linking Asiwa and Bekwai. When the results were released, only ten out of thirty-four students passed, which was a bad record for the school.

When I was in middle form four, I lived in my paternal family's house in Asiwa during the week so I could attend the night studies organized by our head teacher. I usually went home to Anyanso during the weekend. We used an Aladdin (tilley) lamp for night studies. At home, the only time I could use the only kerosene lamp in the house was when everyone else was asleep. Our room was not even cemented. There was no bed or mattress, and sleeping on mats on the floor was the only option for us.

One of the memorable events in my middle school life was when our head teacher, Mr. Attuah, gave me and another boy named Okyere about twenty lashes of the cane. It so happened that we were given six holes to fill with black soil (*humus*) in the school garden so that our head teacher could transplant some pepper and garden-egg seedlings during the break from the morning session. In the course of filling our holes, this boy, who had been intimidating me all the time, stamped on one of the holes I had already filled. I retaliated, and we kept stamping on each other's holes until the ground became hardened. When we were tired, we covered our mess and left for home. When our head teacher came to do the transplanting, he discovered that two holes had been hardened, and he marked those, holes believing we had filled them with red soil against his instructions. When we came back from recess, we were all asked to stand by our holes. He spotted the two of us, and without asking any questions, he grabbed us and gave us about twenty lashes of the cane. Thereafter, we had to remove the soil and refill the holes. The use of the cane as corporal punishment in schools is now something of the past, but in our day, it was a common practice.

During the early 1960s, Dr. Kwame Nkrumah, then president of Ghana, introduced free text books and stationery supplies in schools. He also established the Ghana Young Pioneer Movement, which was later institutionalized in all pretertiary institutions. At the morning assembly, we would recite the national pledge, sing the national anthem, and recite the pioneer pledge. As pioneers, we were taught some patriotic songs and the principles of the young pioneer, which included but were not limited to patriotism, self-discipline, hard work, respect to authority, and safeguarding state property. At the same time, we were being subjected to indoctrination. One of the songs of the young pioneer was "Nkrumah Never Dies, He Forever Lives." At that young age, we could not really understand whether it was his message or his physical being that would never die.

With Opoku Jackson in a secondary school, the rest of the Big Six took the Common Entrance Examination in form four. The examination center was at the Konongo-Odumasi Secondary School, about thirty miles from Asiwa. I was sitting in the front seat just beside the entrance, and close to me was the policeman guarding the examination. As a rural boy, the only time I saw a policeman was when he was coming to make arrests either of basic rate defaulters or those who had committed criminal offenses. The nearest police station to my village was at Yapessa, about fifteen miles away. With this policeman so close to me throughout the examination period, I became nervous, but I managed to finish the examination. When the results were released, I had passed but was unsure that my parents could afford the payment of school fees in a secondary school. At the time secondary school began for the year, I was still at home, thinking of joining my friends in cooperative farmwork (*nnoboa*).

My father was a tailor. He also weaved metal fishing traps, so I used to accompany him to the surrounding villages to sell his products, especially on Saturday and Sunday and during break periods. This activity went on even in my secondary school days. Working on the farm was a daily routine except on Sunday.

In the course of weeding, one cannot escape cutlass cuts or wounds from thorns. Occasionally, I would come across a snake, and I had to be courageous enough to kill it in order to avoid being haunted by it. Sometimes we, the boys, would form a cooperative group, taking turns assisting at each other's farms. This cemented our bond of friendship, as we played together and sometimes ate together at our friends' homes. At other times, we would quarrel among ourselves, especially when someone cheated while playing marbles. Rural life is always community life, and people felt concerned by whatever went on even if it didn't involve a relative or family member.

Knowing very well that my parents had limited resources, when I completed my middle school education, I did not envision any secondary school education in my future. What I had in mind was to join the other teenagers in farming, as this was the only work in the village.

CHAPTER 3

POSTPRIMARY EDUCATION

Secondary School

I completed my middle school education in 1964, but with my parents' financial predicament, I had no vision of a secondary school education. I once told my father to buy me a small cutlass so that I could join my friends in cooperative work (*nnoboa* in Akan language), not knowing what my father had in store for me. One day in September, my father told me that we would go to Kumasi the following Monday. It was an exhilarating piece of news to me, because I had never been to Kumasi before. The only time I passed through Kumasi was when we were going to take our Middle School Leaving Certificate Examination at Bekwai.

On the appointed date, I accompanied my father to Kumasi, and my feeling of happiness was unimaginable. We went to the mission house of the Ahmadiyya Movement at Asafo, a neighborhood in Kumasi. The missionary in charge was Mr. Abdul Wahid, who was my father's friend. I did not actually know whether they had talked before our arrival.

We followed this missionary to the Ahmadiyya Secondary

School, where the missionary sought admission for me. I was dumbfounded, because my father never informed me any of this would be happening. Having completed the admission process, my father took me to some interesting places. We returned the following day. However, a new chapter had opened in my life.

I started my secondary school education at T.I. AMASS in Kumasi on Tuesday, September 28, 1964. The school was established by the Ahmadiyya Muslim Mission of Ghana on January 30, 1950. The first headmaster was Dr. S.B. Ahmad, an expatriate. Initially, there was a student population of twenty-five and seven tutors. The school originally started with two classrooms belonging to the Ahmadiyya Primary School at Asafo, a neighborhood in Kumasi. In 1953 it moved to its present location, Dadiesoaba, another nearby neighborhood in Kumasi. In 1956 the school, which was run as a private school by the Ahmadiyya Movement, was absorbed into the public system. It presented its first batch of candidates for the General Certificate of Education Ordinary Level Examination (G.C.E. O' level) in 1954 and recorded a 100 percent passing rate. Since then, the forward match of the school in academic and other fields began and has continued to this day. Currently, the school has a teaching staff of 132, made up of 107 males and 25 females. The student population is 3,107, with 1,985 boys and 1,122 girls. (source: Headmaster Alhaj Yakub A.B. Abubakar's report on the Sixty-Third Speech and Prize-Giving Day, February 16, 2013)

As a mission school established by the Ahmadiyya Muslim Mission, the school has maintained its enviable record of religious tolerance. "Nobody is compelled to join or practice a religious act that does not agree with his faith. There is no discrimination during admissions nor are other faiths discriminated against in the school. The school offers both the Muslim prayer, Al-Fatihah (the Opening prayer) and The Lord's Prayer (Christian prayer) at every morning assembly as well as any other school gathering since its establishment" (source: Ibid).

Christian personalities like "Rt. Rev. Dr. Sam Prempeh and Rt. Rev. Dr. Yaw Frimpong Manso, both former Moderators of the Presbyterian Church of Ghana, among others, were past students of the school. What the school, however, does not countenance on are acts that will defeat the purpose for which the school was established in the name of religious worship. Such unwelcome acts are corrected appropriately" (source: Sixty-Third Speech and Prize-Giving Day Brochure, February 13, 2013). As a past student and a former tutor of the school, it is a factual statement that the non-Muslim population of the school has always been higher than the Muslim population, but both have lived in peace over the years.

On my first day of school, our English-language tutor, Mr. Ishmail B.K. Addo, asked us to introduce ourselves. As soon as I mentioned my name, Srekye Abubakar, my teacher started laughing. Thereafter, he told me that the correct name is Sadik and not Srekye. There and then, I went to the office to effect the change. The headmaster of the school by then was Mr. M. Latif, an expatriate who administered the school from 1963 to 1969. Mr. Nasir Abdullah Boateng, the first Ghanaian headmaster, followed from 1970 to 1981. Thereafter, Yusuf K. Effah became the headmaster from 1981 to 1990. Mr. Ibrahim K. Gyasi, the first past student, headed the school from1990 to 1998. Mr. Yusuf K. Agyare became the headmaster from 1999 to 2010. Currently, Alhaj. Yakub A. B. Abubakar is the head of the school. All were past students.

Challenges

As a day student, I lived with my aunt Madam Abena Asubonteng who was a plantain seller at the Asafo market. She had lived in Kumasi for a number of years. We were living at House Number

B.H.112 in Asafo, a neighborhood in Kumasi. There were five of us in a single room, all women with the exception of me. They were my aunt Abena Asubonteng and her daughters, Mary Bekoe and Paulina Bekoe. The others were my younger cousins, Amina and Akosua Frema.

It is customary that relatives living in the cities and towns encourage younger family members in the villages to live with them to either go to secondary or technical institutions or to learn a trade. On some occasions when we received relatives from the village, which was very often, I had to join the other boys sleeping on the verandah. After some time, there were so many of us that the verandah became a permanent sleeping place. During the evenings when I had to do my homework and we received a visitor, I had to vacate the room.

After about a year, one resident of the house named Papa Attah (Joseph Attah Tawiah) told my aunt that I could join his nephews and sleep in his hall (living room). He was using a chamber and a hall, and none of his wives were living with him. It was a breather for me but could not solve the problem I had with my night studies. The house was so noisy that no part of the building was suitable for studies. Sometimes I had to walk about two miles to Ahmadiyya Secondary School for my night studies and to work on my assignments. Papa Attah had confidence in me to the extent that he gave me his wardrobe key, despite the presence of his sons and nephews. Papa Attah was once a relatively rich man, a former manager of United African Company (UAC) store in Kumasi, but he had lost his property, including a story building in Kumasi like my father, to defray the debt he incurred through chieftaincy litigation.

When I returned from school in the afternoon, I had to go to Asafo market to my aunt to buy the essentials for the day's meals. While she went around buying the food items, I would sell plantains on her behalf. Thereafter, I would bring the items home on foot about two miles, by which time my younger cousin Amina would have returned from school. She was in the middle school by then. She would prepare the meals, and I would pound the fufu. I was so helpful that everyone who lived in the house liked me. I offered my services to any person who requested it, so food was not a problem for me.

After meals at about seven o'clock, I had to go and wait in line for water from the nearby public tap for the night's use. After all these activities I would become exhausted so much so that I could neither revise my notes nor do my homework, because I easily felt sleepy whenever I picked up my book. In the morning I woke up at about five o'clock to get in line for water for our use before leaving for school. I then had to walk about thirty or forty minutes to reach school by seven o'clock so I could do my schoolwork before lessons started.

During school breaks, I returned to my village to assist my parents on the farm. One day as I was returning from the farm with my head load on a weedy footpath wearing just slippers, I felt a very sharp bite at my heels. I thought it was a bite from a giant ant, so I put down my load to take it off. To my surprise, I saw bloodstains; I then realized that it might be a snake bite. I continued on my way with my load but began feeling dizzy. At one point I had to defecate somewhere in the bush and vomited as well. I became a bit relieved after that and managed to reach home. I informed my mother of my plight. My mother hurriedly gave me some palm oil to mitigate the effect of the poison and later took me to the village medicine man who gave me some concoction to drink. Fortunately for me, it was not one of the most poisonous snakes. One week after the incident, my mother took me back to the village medicine man who removed the fangs of the snake from my leg.

On February 24, 1966, it was announced that President Kwame Nkrumah with his Convention Peoples Party (CPP) government had been overthrown by a military coup d'état. Military and police personnel paraded in their trucks through the main streets in the cities. It was a momentous occasion for those people whose relatives had been detained by Nkrumah's government. I used to visit the Kumasi Central Prison on Saturdays to witness the detainees who were being released from prison. As a result of the change of government, some state institutions established by Nkrumah were either abolished or restructured. My elder brother Hakeem Agyei Twum, who was then working with the Cocoa Marketing Board at Takoradi, lost his job. He had been helping me out by sending a few cedis (the currency of Ghana) to me at the end of every month. That help vanished.

On May 4, 1966, my dear mother, Madam Serah Adwoa Fowaa, died after a short illness. As a student, I was not informed of her death. I received a message that my mother was very sick, so I decided to take a weekend to visit home. She had seen me off to school just a week earlier. Upon reaching home, I saw the entire house in mourning clothes. I wept bitterly and was joined by my father, family members, and other mourners. My mother had died and had already been buried. On April 24, 1967, my elder sister Amina also died.

At the end of my second year in secondary school, I realized from my final grades that my performance was deteriorating. However, I managed to advance to form three the following academic year. Form three in those years was considered as the junior ordinary (O) level in the school, because that was the time for us to choose our subjects for O-level examinations. If one failed to perform well at that grade level one would be repeated.

As my living conditions never got better and my academic performance continued to deteriorate, I was made to repeat the class. In the course of the year, I became so frustrated that I once pleaded with my father to allow me to go to the Teacher Training College where there was free tuition and the students received some allowance, but my father declined my request. He then decided to send me to the boarding house the following year, even though I knew he did not have the resources.

The boarding house was a big relief to me with regard to my studies, but it also created another problem: school fees. I could never pay my fees in full and was almost always sent home for fees. Any time I was sent home, my father would make me accompany him to some moneylenders in the village for a loan. Ironically, those moneylenders never sent any of their children to any secondary school. In some cases, my elder brother Hakeem and my sisters Madina and Fatima would assist my father with whatever amount they could raise, sometimes by selling their sheep and goats. I must state that I am morally obligated to reciprocate their kind gesture during their old age or by assisting their children. Though I am not in Ghana, I do perform that obligation by sending some pittance to them. Later on, my father appealed to my aunts, Madam Amma Donkor and Amma Konadu, for assistance from the proceeds of the family cocoa farm at Saponso, a farming cottage. The farm was a joint project among my uncle Yaw Kyei, my mother Adwoa Fowaa, and her sisters Amma Donkor and Amma Konadu. Saponso was about twenty miles of footpath from Anyanso through farmlands and other villages.

As a teenager, we used to accompany our parents to Saponso during the long school breaks to assist in the harvesting of cocoa. Having lost his job at the Cocoa Marketing Board, my elder brother Hakeem became the custodian of the cocoa farm. Any time I was driven home from school for fees, usually during midterm breaks, I would leave for Anyanso on Friday, and then on Saturday I would make the twenty-mile walk from Anyanso to Saponso. If my brother had some money at home, he would give me some; otherwise, he would have to borrow some money from the purchasing clerk. I would return to Anyanso on Sunday and leave for Kumasi the next day. On Tuesday, I would pay my fees before attending classes.

In some of these instances when I missed the only wooden vehicle in my village from Kumasi, I would take any available vehicle bound for Konongo and wait for the truck at the main junction to our village. Sometimes, some of us would risk our lives by sitting on the roof or hanging onto the battens of the truck to get to our village. Occasionally, the truck would break down on the road, and we would have to continue the rest of the journey on foot, reaching home after midnight.

As soon as school dismissed, I had to travel to my village to help my parents on the farm. In August 1968 while on vacation, my elder brother Zakariya became sick, and my father bought some over-the-counter medications for him, as there was no clinic in the village. One morning he woke up, and his condition had become very critical so my father decided to take him to Achiase clinic. Achiase was about six miles from my village, and the only truck in my village had already left for Kumasi.

At about nine thirty in the morning, my father requested assistance from family members and friends to help transport him to Achiase. As village life is a community life, people willingly assist in such critical conditions. An improvised stretcher was made to carry my brother. A big cloth was tied to the ends of two pestles. He was then put inside the cloth, and four people carried him on their shoulders. When they became tired, another set of people took over. When we got to the clinic, he was given some treatment, but the nurse on duty recommended that he was to be taken to Agogo Presbyterian Hospital for further treatment. My father hired a truck at Achiase at about four o'clock that same afternoon and took him to Agogo Hospital where he underwent a successful surgery. He remained at Agogo for more than a month before being discharged.

Sometimes I had to clear a piece of land with my late older brother Zakariya for farming to generate some income for our upkeep at school. He was then attending Kanton Teacher Training College at Tumu in the upper east region of Ghana. On November 17, 1969, when I was in the first term of form five in secondary school, I received the bad news of the death of my dear father, Sadik Bosompem. After his death, the burden of my education fell on the shoulders of my aunts Amma Donkor and Amma Konadu, who were determined to let me complete my secondary school education. My brother Hakeem and my sisters Madina and Fatima also continued to assist in funding my secondary school education.

While in secondary school, I was taking care of one of my sister's cocoa farms during the long breaks. The main cocoa season falls between June and September, which coincided with the long break. I weeded the farm, plucked the ripe cocoa pods, opened the pods for the beans, covered them for fermentation, brought the beans home for drying, and finally sent the dried beans off for sale at the cocoa depot. All this I did with friends in the form of cooperative work.

In spite of the difficulties that I encountered during my secondary school education, I was a happy boy in my own world. I was privileged for being one of the very few in my village at the time to attend secondary school. Thus, I had my fair share of serious flirtation with some local girls, exhibiting my youthful exuberance.

T.I. AMASS had a unique situation that many people did not recognize. It was the only Muslim secondary school at the time in Ghana and was situated in the heart of the city within walking distance to and from the central business district of Kumasi. The school was unfenced and was very close to the Kumasi Sports Stadium with a lot of attractions and distractions. For example, there were numerous nightclubs in the Amakom and Asafo neighborhoods compared to its contemporaries in the city, such as Prempeh College, Opoku Ware Secondary School, Yaa Asantewaa, and St. Louis Secondary Schools, which were all far away from the city. Notwithstanding these unfortunate situations, the school compared favorably with its peers in academics and sports, which it has maintained consistently.

Our exciting moments as students were during the annual interschool and college sports competitions. We competed with such institutions as Prempeh College, Opoku Ware Secondary School, Wesley College, Kumasi Polytechnic, Konongo-Odumase Secondary School, Akrokerri Teacher Training College, and Obuasi Secondary Technical School. The girls' institutions included, but were not limited to, Yaa Asantewaa and St. Louis Secondary Schools, Juaben Women's Training College, and a host of others. It was an interesting spectacle.

With our proximity advantage to the stadium, AMASS students would flock to the sports stadium to cheer for our teams. Though the school had very few girls compared to boys, the girls competed very well against the other girls' institutions. One female student named Habiba Atta solely scored many points for the school, competing in both track and field events with excellence. Sometimes, there would be clashes between some of the institutions at the stadium, which is a common feature of sports anywhere.

In his report at the Sixty-Third Speech and Prize-Giving Day Celebration of the school, the headmaster, Alhaj Yakub A.B. Abubakar, said, "The School still maintains its excellence in academics and sports as well as discipline. The School is currently occupying the enviable position of being the six times running Super Zonal Champions (Boys and Girls) in the whole Ashanti Region, which has over one-hundred and twenty Senior High Schools."

I completed my secondary school education in June 1970. Unfortunately, when the results were released in the early week of September 1970, it was announced that some papers had been thrown out by the West African Examinations Council due to an examination leakage. The subjects involved were English Language, Mathematics, Geography, Akan (Asante Twi), and History—five of the seven subjects that I offered for my final examination. We had to retake those parts of the test in November of the same year, which adversely affected my overall results.

While waiting for the results of the test I'd retaken, I applied for appointment as an uncertificated teacher at the District Education Office at Bekwai. On February 15, 1971, I received my appointment letter from the District Education Office posting me to Nsuta Local Authority Primary School, otherwise known as Adomkrom (Nsuta), which is a farming community about eighteen miles east of New Edubiase in the Adansi District of Ashanti.

The school was located in Nsuta, which happened to be centralized and larger than the other farming communities. The students had to come from the surrounding communities and converged at Nsuta. It was also the marketing center. Sundays were the market days where people from far and near did their trading activities. The school had just four teachers with fourth and fifth grades combined due to poor enrolment. My monthly salary at the time was thirty-three cedis.

The journey from New Edubiase to Nsuta was a very difficult one. The road was so deplorable that only tractors and timber trucks could use it, and in some cases, we had to make the eighteen-mile journey on foot. At the end of the academic year, I was transferred to Aframoase Local Authority Primary School as the head teacher. Aframoase was about ten miles from Nsuta. Unlike Nsuta, the road to Aframoase was just a footpath through cocoa farms. Prior to the end of the academic year, in August 1971, I had applied for admission to the Bagabaga Teacher Training College for my Postsecondary Teachers' Certification Course.

Teacher Training College

On September 15, 1971, I received a letter from Bagabaga Teacher Training College in Tamale, Northern Ghana, that I should attend an interview at Wesley College in Kumasi. On the date scheduled for the interview, I made myself available, and fortunately, I was successful. I then made preparations for my Teacher Training College education. When I received my September salary, I bought all the necessary items and left for Tamale on October 10, 1971, the reopening date.

Bagabaga Teacher Training College, now the University of Development Studies, was then composed of the Agricultural Science Specialist Department, Rural Science Department, and the Postsecondary Department. The Postsecondary Department was mainly men, but during my time there, it was made coeducational. It was my first time traveling to the northern part of Ghana, so I really enjoyed the journey from Kumasi. The vegetation was quite different from that found in the middle belt of tropical woodland. Unfortunately, on our way, the State Transport Setra Bus we were traveling on had its fan belt torn out, and we needed water to fill the tank to restore the cooling system. We spent more than an hour to get some water from somewhere before we could continue the journey.

The first problem that I faced was the weather. Tamale, and for that matter, the northern region, has drier weather. From November to early March, northern Ghana experiences the harmattan, a dry, hot wind that blows sand from the Sahara Desert. One day as I was returning from classes, I spotted blood on my shirt, and when I inquired, I was told that it was due to the weather changes. We also faced the problem of water supply. But on the whole, I was very happy because I happened to meet four of my secondary school mates and also made some new friends.

At the Teacher Training College, the education was free, so I did not face any financial difficulties as compared to my secondary school days. In addition, those of us from southern Ghana were given twenty cedis per term as a transportation allowance. The fare from Kumasi to Tamale by then was three cedis, so we could get some extra money for some other expenses.

During Christmas break, I came to my village. On Tuesday December 28, 1971, as I was playing a football with my friends on the football field, I collided with the late Kwaku Dwuma who was in the goalpost, and he fell on me. As a result, I had a fracture of my left leg and had to be carried home. This injury made me stay at home for the whole second term of my first year in Teacher Training College. I received traditional treatment for more than three months. When college reopened for the third term, I joined my colleagues for classes. This meant that I had missed the first practical teaching, which was and still is a prerequisite for receiving a teacher's certificate. However, I participated in the remaining three practical teachings.

During my second year of college in 1973, I registered for the General Certificate of Education O-level examination to better my grades in English Language and Mathematics before writing my final Teacher Training College Examination. As a member of the Geographical Society of the college, we embarked on a one-week field trip from Tamale in the northern region to the south of Ghana, visiting such places as the Tema Harbor, Lome in the Republic of Togo, Elmina and Cape Coast castles, as well as the Takoradi Harbor.

On August 17, 1972, when I was on break, I was awakened from sleep by a sudden noise from relatives crying and wailing in the house, so I got up to find out what was happening. To my utter surprise, I was informed that one of my cousins named Charles Kyei Baffour, popularly known as Kofi Charles, had died. I hurriedly prepared myself and headed for Nsuaem, a footpath journey of about eight miles, walking in the night with the help of a lantern and flashlight. Charles was very dear to me, because anytime that I went to Nsuaem, he was my companion. Though a bit older than me, we did everything together. He had just completed his bachelor's degree from the University of Cape Coast. His death was a big blow to the entire family and community.

The practice of the teacher training institutions was that during the last term, students would fill out applications for the schools where they wanted to work. Sometimes, an application would be sent to a district you did not even choose, depending on the priority of the region. Eventually, when I received my posting, I had been posted to my own village, Anyanso.

By July 31, we had all finished our final examinations and left for our various towns. On August 20, I received my appointment letter from the Bekwai District Education Office. I presented my appointment letter to the head teacher of the school. On September 18, 1973, when school reopened, I reported for duty as a full-fledged certified post-secondary school teacher.

CHAPTER 4

CAREER AS A TEACHER

A Teacher in My Village

When school reopened on Tuesday, September 18, 1973, I reported for duty. The head teacher of the school was Mr. Gyamfi Kumaning who had just been transferred to head the school. My elder brother, the late Adjei Zakariya, had also been transferred to the school. Mr. Kwaku Dwamena was the only teacher who had been in the school the previous year. The former head teacher had requested to be transferred, and the remaining two teachers had been transferred at the request of the community.

As the only postsecondary teacher and the youngest among the postprimary teachers, I was posted to the form four middle school classroom, which was an examination class. We worked solidly together to build the image of the school, which had been tarnished by the previous teachers due to absenteeism and lack of commitment to their work. We did our best to instill discipline and improve academic work in the school. We organized friendly football and netball matches among the neighboring schools at Anyinase, Asiwa, Anumso, Achiase, Nsuaem, Asante Ofoase, and Danso. We expanded the school's playing field and constructed a netball field for the girls. Two years later, Mr. Dwamena left the school on transfer, and Mr. Osei Agyeman replaced him.

Marriage

In January 1976, I married my dear wife, Mary Akosua Tenewaa, a former student of the school. The traditional practice, especially in the rural communities, is that parents felt honored when their daughters were formally requested in marriage before consummation. After my older sister Fatima had finished the preliminary requests from both parents, we performed the traditional marriage rites on both the father's and the mother's side. The daughter of Opanin Ali Kwaku Addae and Alice Adoma (Akosua Ataa), a young lady who had won the respect of the people for her honesty, patience, calmness, hard work, and, above all, respect for elders and peers alike. She has a lone brother, Simon Kofi Mensah, and three younger sisters, Rose Amoah (Akua Sikayena), Janet Abena Amoah (Abena Addae), and Elizabeth Amaniampong. Her late grandmother Afia Serwaa (Amaneamahunu) was a very industrious woman. She owned a chain of cocoa farms and farmlands, making her one of the wealthy residents of the village.

As marriage is a bond between not only the couple but also the two families, there was, and still is, a good relationship between our families. I recognized her younger siblings as my own children. Those relationships still exist till now, though they are all married people. We had our first daughter, Hanna Yaa Boampomaa Aboagye, in December that same year at Achiase maternity clinic.

An Ordeal

Barely three months after delivery, my wife contracted a prolonged health problem. As I was returning from the mosque after morning prayers one dawn, I heard people yelling and rushing toward my wife's residence, so I also rushed to the scene. To my utter surprise, I saw my wife lying unconscious in a pool of water. The practice in the rural communities where there are no health facilities was to resuscitate an unconscious person by pouring a lot of water on the person. After some time, she regained consciousness.

The only wooden vehicle in my village had left for Kumasi and would not return till dusk. People helped, especially her elder brother Kofi Simon, to carry her on their backs to the nearby clinic at Ofoase in the Asante-Akim district, which was about three miles away from our village. The dispenser at the clinic gave her some treatment. She stayed at Ofoase for one week before she was discharged. During this one week, I had to shuttle daily from Anyanso to Ofoase either in the morning before school or in the evening after school. This incident affected me psychologically and in my work, because until I had visited her, I would not be very sure of her condition as it was on and off.

One week after she was discharged from clinic, she had not fully recovered, and this time I had to take her to the Ahmadiyya Hospital at Asokore about forty miles away from our village. After examination, the doctor prescribed malaria treatment for her. As a teacher, I could not stay with her throughout the days but made periodic visits. Her mother was taking care of her and sent her to the hospital anytime she felt sick. She was discharged from the hospital after ten days of treatment, and I went to Asokore to bring her back to Anyanso.

When we reached Kumasi in the afternoon, our only wooden vehicle had gone for regular maintenance so we had to wait till it returned. As we were waiting at the terminal, I told them I was going to the market to buy a few essentials. When we were waiting, her temperature rose so high that I rushed her to the Komfo Anokye Hospital where she was given malaria treatment and discharged. At this point, I was at my wits' end and did not know what to do. Fortunately, we were able to catch our only wooden vehicle to the village.

We left Kumasi at about six o'clock in the evening. In the truck, she lay on my lap while our daughter was with my wife's mother. As she lay on my lap, I could feel that her body was very cold, as if she had swum in the river for a long time or she had taken a very long shower. At that moment, my only hope and prayer was in God Almighty for her survival. When we reached Anyanso, the driver stopped the vehicle in front of their residence. When we got down, people started wailing when they heard the news that she had not fully recovered, signaling that there was no hope for her survival. After all these medical treatments had failed to yield any fruitful results, her parents approached my family to try some other traditional treatments.

For about three months, I passed through a period of psychological trauma. At times I felt that I was not of myself as I stood in front of my class, because sometimes I had to be called from the classroom when it occurred. She was taken to various places, but they returned with conflicting results. All these times, she was taking her medications and making periodic visits to the hospital. Eventually, she recovered from that prolonged malaria sickness after about three months of shuttling between hospitals and traditional treatments.

At this juncture, I would like to acknowledge the support, cooperation, and encouragement of my family members, that of my wife, fellow teachers, and friends during this period of bizarre experience. I passed through the turmoil of a financial, physical, and psychological nature, but with God's grace, everything came to an end with my wife and child surviving. Since then, she has never been hospitalized even for a day, except for minor aches and periodic checkups.

As a village teacher, I combined farming with my professional work to supplement my income, including weeding, felling trees, setting fire to the dried weeds, and clearing the land for cultivation. At times, I had to rush to the farm after the close of school at four o'clock in the evening. Saturday and Sunday were busy farming days with little time to rest. Holidays were even busier for farming activities. There were times when we used the school children on our farms. Fetching water and firewood for the teachers was and is an agelong practice in some rural schools. Overexploitation of the students usually incurred the displeasure and anger of the community, thus bringing a rift between the school and the community. In some extreme cases, reports were made to the District Education Office, and the teachers concerned could be penalized, including being transferred.

Working in one's own community can sometimes be very challenging. The four years that I taught in my village had mixed results. As a young man receiving a monthly salary in a predominantly farming community, girls and some parents tried to lure me into marrying them or their daughters. Some girls were always making seductive greetings and movements. Among my friends and other peers, I seemed exceptional or fortunate to be a salary earner.

Community Work

For the four years I spent in my village, I was the secretary of the Town Development Committee. Sometimes I became a subject of controversy, especially when a new bylaw was enacted and implemented for the governance of the community or when communal labor defaulters were arraigned before the chief. The recalcitrant ones were arrested by the police, and the secretary incurred the wrath of the affected people or their parents.

Combining my schoolwork, the community work, farmwork, and other family duties made my work very difficult, but I managed to excel as much as I could. As the secretary of the committee, I was responsible for commuting between my village and the office of the district chief executive for the supply of the community's share of the materials for development projects. As there was no direct road linking Anyanso to the district capital of Bekwai, I had to pass through Kumasi to get to Bekwai. When I was not fortunate enough to get the only vehicle back to my village, I had to board any available vehicle to any nearby village and continue the rest of the journey on foot, sometimes walking for about ten miles at night. My flashlight was my best companion.

On October 2, 1975, I applied for a change of name through the District Education Office from Sadik Abubakar to Sadik Aboagye Bosompem to reflect my tribal identity. Two months later, I received a letter from the Director General of the Ghana Teaching Service effecting the change of name. I decided to apply for a transfer to another station in 1976 after three years of service in my village. My request was denied by the District Education Officer on the grounds that I was teaching an examination class and could not get the transfer in the middle of the academic year. I stayed and resolved to spend four years to be eligible for a release from the district. For the four years I taught the examination class, the overall results were very encouraging as compared to the previous years' records.

Teaching at Asokore

I was eager to pursue further education, so in April 1977, I applied for a release from the Bekwai Education District. As a condition for the release, I had to present an assurance letter from my prospective employer. I did this by traveling to the headquarters of the Ahmadiyya Education Unit at Saltpond on two occasions. I was granted the release from the district when I presented the assurance letter to the district education officer at Bekwai. I presented my release letter to the headquarters of the Ahmadiyya Education Unit at Saltpond. I was posted to the Ahmadiyya Middle School in Asokore in the Sekyere District of Ashanti.

In September 1977, I started work at the T.I. Ahmadiyya Middle School at Asokore. I was assigned to the form three classroom. The existing teachers were Mr. Mensah, the head teacher; Mr. Bonsu, mathematics specialist teacher; Mr. Sekyere; and Ms. Matilda. Mensah The school lacked discipline. The following academic year 1978/79 I took my students to form four classroom.

That year I met Mr. Abdullah Mahmud Sam who was posted to the school, but after just one term, he was transferred to Kumasi. I tried harder to get my students to learn to pass their final examination, but it proved futile. The students were not prepared to learn, especially the final-year students. Many of them failed to attend the early-morning and night classes that were organized for them. The practice in the area was that some head teachers, including our own, would collect some money from the students to sway the invigilators into allowing the students to cheat at the final examinations. So passing an examination was just a formality. Just present yourself at the examination center, and you were sure to pass.

The head teacher left the school in midterm, and Mr. Kwaku Bonsu had to take over for him. We did our best to persuade the students to put in some extra effort to study, but they would not. Unfortunately for this batch of students, the examination was conducted under very strict supervision. Reports of examination malpractice in the Effiduase-Asokore area had reached the West Africa Examinations Council, so that particular year, the council dispatched more police personnel who cordoned off the examination premises. The head teachers had no access to the premises to influence the invigilators. The examination results in the area for that year were abysmally poor. Out of the twenty-three students presented by our school, only one student, Asenso Michael, was able to pass the final examination.

In September 1978, my wife gave birth to our second child named Sadik Kwadwo Bosompem Aboagye at Anyanso while I was at Asokore. My wife was stationed at Anyanso doing farming, while I paid periodic visits to them. They joined me for a brief period in Asokore. During the latter part of the 1978/79 academic year, I made up my mind to leave Asokore either to further my education or to join the exodus of teachers to Nigeria. I had already applied for admission to the University of Ghana–Accra, for a diploma in the Study of Religions and Philosophy. At the same time, I was working on my passport for my intended travel to Nigeria.

In May 1979, I received a letter from the University of Ghana to write an examination and attend an interview at the same time. By the end of July 1979, I had received a letter of admission from the university. I then abandoned my intended travel to Nigeria and accepted the offer by the university. It turned out to be a very good decision.

In August 1979, I traveled with my friend Ayub Agyekum, now deceased, who had just completed his bachelor's degree in Political Science at the University of Ghana, to pay for my admission fees. He was the first university graduate in my village. That was the heightened period of the Armed Forces Revolutionary Council (AFRC) uprising, and there was an acute shortage of fuel that affected transportation. We had to walk for about twenty miles from Anyanso to Bomfa junction, the main junction joining the Kumasi-Accra truck road. From there, we were happy to get an articulated truck to Nkawkaw. We could not get any vehicle to continue our journey to Accra. At that moment, there was a heavy downpour of rain at Nkawkaw.

The rain subsided at about six o'clock in the evening. We then decided to go to Mpraeso on the mountains to lodge with Ayub Agyekum's younger cousin, Okyere, also now deceased. We did not get any vehicle either so we joined other travelers on foot to climb the mountain, a distance of more than seven miles. By the time we arrived at Mpraeso, we were wet to the skin. We spent the night there, and on the following morning, we continued our journey on a tipper truck from Mpraeso to Nkawkaw. Upon reaching Nkawkaw, we had another articulated truck heading for Accra after waiting for more than two hours. We reached Accra after seven o'clock that evening. We lodged with one of his friends at the university's campus. We returned the following day. Now that I had paid my admission fees, I was just waiting for the reopening of the university.

University of Ghana

On the September 10, 1979, I reported at the University of Ghana–Legon to start my university education. I was allocated a room at C32 Mensah Sarbah Hall, and my roommate was Joe Nyarko, a business administration student and a resident of Kumasi. I was reading a diploma course in the Study of Religions and Philosophy.

While at the university, my two children were simultaneously attacked by the deadly disease known as measles, but my elder brother Zakariya, now deceased, assisted my wife and took them to the hospital for treatment. The two years that I studied at the university, Ghanaians were passing through difficult times due to the June 4 uprising in the military, led by Flight Lieutenant Jerry John Rawlings. At the university, students had to wait in lines at the central cafeteria and at the various residence halls for meals. Essential commodities like sugar, milk, rice, flour, and other basic food items were difficult to come by.

On completion of my studies at University of Ghana–Legon, I was posted to the Ashanti Region for my national service assignment. When I went for my posting at the Regional Education Office in Kumasi, I discovered that I had been posted to the Wesley College, which was a Christian institution. I informed the posting officer that my option was Islamic studies and not Christian studies. I was later posted to T.I. AMASS. That same year, a new headmaster had been posted to the school in the person of Mr. Yusuf K. Effah. I shared one room with my cousin Asare James for some time until the school offered me an accommodation. I was assigned to forms two and three for Islamic studies and sixth form for Islamic studies and African traditional religion. On January 30, 1982, Mr. Y.K. Effah inaugurated the Parent-Teacher Association of T.I. AMASS with the late Alhaj V.A. Essaka as the chairman. An amount of four thousand cedis was realized from the fundraising activity.

On March 1, 1982, I sent my son Hamid Akwasi Kyei Aboagye to the Methodist Hospital in the village of Amakom near Lake Bosomtwe for the treatment of measles. He had been sent to some other clinics for treatment with no improvement. On March 11, 1982, he passed away at the hospital. He was eleven months old.

With the completion of my one year of national service at the end of August 1982, I planned to travel to Nigeria to join the exodus of Ghanaian teachers and other professionals. The living conditions in Ghana at the time were hopeless and frustrating.

Salaries of workers were woefully inadequate for most of the people with families. Basic essential commodities of life like milk, sugar, soap, rice, and other foodstuffs were very difficult to come by. Petroleum products were equally scarce, thus creating a situation of hoarding of such items by traders, which resulted in higher prices. That also created an avenue for some unscrupulous people to cheat others to enrich themselves. It was not surprising that a lot of Ghanaians, professional and nonprofessional alike, trooped to Nigeria for a better life.

Chapter 5

Sojourn in Nigeria

The Journey to Nigeria

On September 15, 1982, my friend Ayub Kusi Agyekum, now deceased, and I left Accra for Lagos, Nigeria. We traveled by road through Togo and Benin Republics. He had been teaching in Nigeria for the past year. As soon as we crossed the border towns of Aflao and Lome, in Ghana and Togo Republics respectively, the situation changed. Essential commodities held as a treasure in Ghana at that time were being openly displayed by traders on the roadside in Togo. There and then I realized why people were traveling outside Ghana for a better life elsewhere, especially Nigeria, which boasted a booming economy. We reached Lagos at night, so we had to sleep in the bus. The next day we went to my friend's village, Imodi-Ijasi, near Ijebu-Ode in Ogun State, where he was the assistant principal of the school where he was teaching.

In Lagos, I observed the wide streets, sometimes three lanes on each side, with overhead bridges popularly called flyovers, comparable to what can be seen in more advanced countries. On September 17, we traveled to Ibadan to visit our old friend Mr.

Abdul Lamidi and also to explore the opportunity of a teaching appointment. I used to stay at Ibadan because my longtime friend Mr. Abdul Lamidi, a native Ibadan resided there. He was a Nigerian born and raised in Ghana. He was a teacher at Anyanso and married a lady there. I stayed with my friend Ayub for about four months, traveling to Ibadan and Abeokuta all in search of a teaching appointment without success. On some occasions, we would travel to Lagos to visit some friends and some interesting places, including the prestigious Ikoyi neighborhood on Lagos Island. Huge bridges connected the Lagos mainland to Lagos Island.

In the course of my travels, I observed very wide rivers like the Niger and Ogun Rivers, as I had never traveled to the eastern part of Nigeria. What was lacking in Ghana at the time was in abundance in Nigeria. Some of the Ghanaians took advantage to further their education in some Nigerian Universities. Others used Nigeria as a stepping stone to travel to either America or some of the European countries. With the Volkswagen assembly plant in Lagos and the Peugeot plant in Kaduna, some Ghanaians were able to purchase their own cars. There were others who worked hard to purchase buses and trucks for transportation businesses either in Nigeria or Ghana.

Deportation

I had searched for a teaching appointment but to no fruition.

To further complicate my situation, the federal government of Nigeria ordered all illegal aliens to leave the country within two weeks on January 17, 1983. This incident reminded me of the Aliens Compliance Order, popularly called the Quit Order, which was promulgated in Ghana by the Progress Party Government led by Dr. Kofi Abrefa Busia in 1970. This instrument by the government sent many aliens back to their home countries, mostly

West African nationals. It was a pathetic situation when some of our alien classmates and roommates had to leave the school midterm. As T.I. MASS is a Muslim institution, a lot of foreign nationals were students in the school, some of whom were my classmates.

The Nigerian federal government order compelled those of us who did not possess the resident permit to leave Nigeria for our various countries—in our case, Ghana. This was a pathetic situation, but we had no option. On January 24, 1983, I joined the hundreds of thousands of Ghanaians at the Apapa Wharf in Lagos for the free ship provided by the Ghana Government. We stayed at the port for two days to no avail. We later learned that the ship had docked at Cotonou in Benin. At noon on January 26, I traveled with one of my nephews, the late Kwasi Afoakwa, to Cotonou to join the thousands of illegal Ghanaians heading for home.

We boarded the ship at two o'clock in the morning on January 27, 1983. It was a struggle for survival, as there were many more people onboard than the ship could carry, especially those who had a lot of luggage. Some of the immigrants hired trucks and buses to travel by road. We reached Tema Port at half past eleven in the morning two days later. We were evacuated from the harbor to the trade fair site where we spent the night. There, I met one of my friends and a citizen of Anyanso, Paul Nkrumah, so we left Accra for Anyanso. We boarded a truck from Accra to Konongo and later took a truck from Konongo up to Obogu in the Asante-Akim District. We had to walk a distance of about twenty miles to reach Anyanso at about ten o'clock at night. My hope and desire to travel to Nigeria to brighten my future and that of my family was truncated by this expulsion order.

Whether this action by the federal government of Nigeria was retaliation to a similar order by the Busia Government of

Ghana some years earlier or a mere coincident, I can never tell. However, we were given a hero's welcome as some of the returning immigrants lost their lives on the way.

Home at Last

Upon reaching home, I heard the good news that my wife had given birth to a baby girl, Aisha Akosua Agyeiwaa Aboagye, earlier in January 1983. I remained at Anyanso for a long period of time. I made up my mind to return to Nigeria to continue my unfulfilled agenda when the situation normalized. In view of that, I did not find any work but rather decided to help my wife with her farming work.

On March 3, 1983, a fire broke out in Anyanso and the surrounding areas, but we later learned that it was a national tragedy, as the outbreak affected most of Ghana. The fire destroyed large tracts of forestland, farm produce, cocoa farms, animals, and property. It was a catastrophe, and the aftermath was drought, severe famine, and poverty.

On June 22, 1983, my aunt Amma Donkor died at the Komfo Anokye Hospital in Kumasi, and the final funeral rites were performed on July 16 and 17, 1983, at Nsuaem.

On August 22, 1983, I was awakened from sleep by my sister Fatima and told me that my nephew Asiedu was dying. He had been attacked by cholera. Fortunately, my friend Mr. Kwadwo Antwi (Bob) had come from Tema to perform the final funeral rites for his father's brother, Opanin Agyapong, who had died on February 1. We pleaded with him to assist us in getting Asiedu to the nearest hospital. Though he had been awake the whole night and in spite of the acute fuel problem in Ghana at the time, he agreed to take us to the nearest hospital, the Mines Hospital at Konongo. Asiedu made it to the hospital where he received treatment. At this point, I should express my heartfelt appreciation to Mr. Kwadwo Antwi for that gesture.

During my stay at Anyanso for a period of about six months, I really tasted life without any source of income. It was a bizarre experience that we went through, but the end result was marvelous as we had a bumper harvest out of our farming activity.

Second Attempt

On September 10, 1983, I traveled with my friend Ayub to Nigeria for the second time. As a teacher in Nigeria, he had to return for duty after his vacation in Ghana. By then, Ghana had closed the border with Togo, so we had to use some unorthodox route through Jasikan in the northern part of the Volta Region. We walked through bushes and farmlands to the northern part of Togo before boarding a bus for Lome in the south. We then continued our journey through Benin to Nigeria. We eventually reached Lagos on the third day and resided at Imodi-Ijasi, near Ijebu-Ode in Ogun where my friend was stationed as a secondary school teacher.

The next day we traveled to Ibadan to visit our friend Mr. Abdul Lamidi and his family. I remained there to explore the possibility of finding a teaching appointment. Thereafter, I shuttled between Ibadan, Abeokuta, and Imodi-Ijasi in search of a teaching appointment. Later I traveled to Kaduna and Kano in the northern states but to no avail. Finally, I settled at Ijebu-Ode and had to content myself with some clerical job of some sort to keep me alive and to further explore the possibility of finding another job. By then, the recruitment of teachers had been closed.

I shared one room with one Amoah Gyimah, a former teacher and a cousin to my friend Ayub. Nigeria had good road network of thousands of miles of expressways linking the major cities and towns. I remember that one day I was traveling to visit a friend named Mr. Brenya who was teaching in another village. I boarded a Toyota Hiace minibus from Ijebo-Ode. I was the lone passenger, and this teenage driver was traveling at a speed of between 120 and 140 miles per hour. No amount of persuasion would convince this young driver to slow down. I heaved a huge sigh of relief when I finally reached my friend's village.

Second Deportation

Once again in May 1985, the federal government issued another order that all illegal immigrants should leave the country within two weeks. I had no option but to join the bandwagon of illegal aliens heading for Ghana. Those of us who for one reason or another could not meet the deadline and got stranded at the Benin border and those yet to reach the border were directed to converge at the Hajj camp at the Murtala Muhammad International Airport. We were kept on tenterhooks at the camp for days amid rain and sunshine as the number kept increasing by thousands each passing day.

Out of frustration, hunger, and thirst the deportees made a demonstration against the police guarding us at the camp. Some threw stones and any other available materials at the police. The police in turn threw tear gas into our midst, releasing fumes and choking us. At times, some of the Ghanaians quickly picked up the tear gas before it exploded and threw it back to the police, causing uneasiness among the police. They also gave warning shots. The demonstrators set five cars and all the posters along the airport road ablaze.

On the fifth day, we were informed that the border had been opened for us to continue our journey back home. We were happy as hundreds of cars, buses, and trucks lined up toward the Benin border, not knowing what was ahead of us. A detachment of the mobile police had mounted a roadblock a few miles away from the border to punish us for the destruction at the Hajj camp. All of us were ordered out of our vehicles and lined up in a single file as we walked through a barricade, and each person had to receive some strokes of the cane. Some were severely beaten, and even a few recalcitrant people were shot dead. Some died out of hunger, thirst, and sickness. I nearly died of hunger, as I was feeling dizzy to the extent that I could no longer bear it. Just one piece of fish and some water at a nearby village saved me. We stayed the night there and continued our journey the following day.

As the temporary gate was opened, hundreds of vehicles headed for Ghana. Some had to board the ship provided by the government of Ghana, while others made it through the Togo border. To further complicate the situation of the returnees, the Ghana side of the Togo border had been closed by the Provisional National Defence Council Government led by Jerry John Rawlings. The closure caused the death of some more Ghanaian returnees. I joined the group that boarded the ship at Cotonou, and it took about three days before we reached Ghana. At the harbor, articulated trucks waited to convey us to our various regional capitals. I reached my village, Anyanso, the next day as my family was expecting me. I was very grateful to God that once again I had reached home in safety and good health.

Later I learned that my cousin Asare James had gotten the opportunity to travel to Libya through a recruitment exercise that Libyan authorities conducted through the Education Ministry for professional teachers to teach in Libya. However, we did communicate through letter writing, because cell phones were not very common at that time. Currently, both of us have emerged in the United States, though in different states. He is in Raleigh, North Carolina, and I am in Chicago, Illinois.

CHAPTER 6

REINSTATEMENT

At T.I. AMASS

In August 1985, I applied for reinstatement into the Ghana Education Service at the Regional Education Office in Kumasi. My former headmaster, Mr. Y.K. Effah, helped me to get posted to the T.I. AMASS as the Islamic studies teacher. I stayed in Kumasi while my wife and children remained at Anyanso. I made periodic visits to them and helped her in her farming activities during breaks and on some weekends.

In May 1986, we gave birth to another child, Serah Akosua Fowaa Aboagye, named after my late dear mother, Serah Adwoa Fowaa. In March 1987 during one of my usual weekend visits to Anyanso, my daughter Agyeiwaa felt sick, and I had to take her to the Agogo Presbyterian Hospital. I went to Anyanso on Friday and took her to the hospital the next day. She was treated and discharged late in the afternoon but her temperature was still very high. I realized that being a Saturday, I might face transportation problems from Konongo to Anyanso. God guided me in my decision to stay with her in the children's room for the night.

At about midnight, she made a wild scream, and soon after, she fell unconscious. I called out to the nurse on duty, and she was rushed to the emergency ward for observation. She was diagnosed and the result was that she had contracted pneumonia. Since the village vehicle did not work on Sundays, I sent a message to my wife the following Monday that she had been admitted. By then, my wife was nursing our newborn daughter, so her mother came the following day to look after Agyeiwaa while I went back to work. She remained hospitalized for more than three months, while I shuttled between Kumasi and Agogo to see how she was responding to treatment and to provide their needs.

In September 1987 I brought my first two children, Hanna and Kwadwo, to live with me in Kumasi. I sent them to the T.I. Ahmadiyya Preparatory School, which was a private institution. After just one year, I transferred them to Ahmadiyya Primary School, a public institution, because the fees at the private school were too high for me. The following year I brought Abena Adane, a niece to my wife, to live with us while my wife and the other children remained at Anyanso.

In July 1988, we brought forth another child, Muhammad Kwasi Boadi Aboagye. My wife and the younger children still remained at Anyanso doing her farming activities. As a hardworking woman, she combined farming with trading in foodstuffs from the village to Kumasi and sometimes to Accra. By doing so, she was able to offer financial and material assistance to her younger sister, Abena Amoah, who was by then an apprentice seamstress in Kumasi. Whenever the two of us left for the village, Abena took care of the children at our residence at Ahmadiyya Secondary School compound. Sometimes, when my wife was unable to travel to Kumasi, Abena took care of the foodstuffs and sold things to the traders in Kumasi. I made periodic visits to them, and she, in turn, made some periodic visits to us in Kumasi.

In August 1988, my friend Mr. Sam paid a four-day visit to my village, Anyanso. In September of that year the landlord who was leasing his building to the school evacuated all the teachers in his rental apartments, so I moved from my apartment to occupy just two rooms on the school compound. I was in the same building with Mr. Abdullah Mahmud Sam. He had been a casual friend since we met in Asokore briefly in 1978, but later our friendship grew so much that we did many things together.

In April 1988 my headmaster, the late Mr. Yusuf K. Effah, appointed me as a substantive housemaster of Nayyar House (House Two). Before then, I was the assistant to one Mr. Moses who went abroad. In August of the same year I was appointed the secretary to the school's Parent-Teacher Association at a general meeting.

On October 21, 1988, I sent my daughter Hanna Aboagye to the University Hospital in Kumasi for chronic coughing. All the medications proved futile until I consulted my former classmate Dr. Muhammad B. Ibrahim who was then working at Okomfo Anokye Teaching Hospital. He gave me a prescription for an x-ray at the Okomfo Anokye Teaching Hospital for possible lung problems. On December 12, 1988, I sent her for the x-ray, and the result showed that her lung was clear. He then prescribed a quantity of antibiotics that cured her. I later realized that she carried a heavy load from the farm at Anyanso and that might have caused her problems.

On January 19, 1990, Mr. Sam gave my wife fifty thousand cedis to supplement her trading in palm oil. In March 1990 my wife and the other children, as well as my nephew Asiedu, finally joined us in Kumasi. My friend Mr. Sam left Kumasi for Accra en route to Kano, Nigeria, at the invitation of his uncle on June 14, 1990. In July we gave birth to yet another child, Abdullah Kwadwo Osam Aboagye. Mr. Sam had left for Kano,

Nigeria, before the child was born. I named this child after him to show my appreciation for his kindness and also to cement our friendship, which had grown from strength to strength ever since.

My First Headmaster, the Late Y.K. Effah

At the end of August 1990, Mr. Y.K. Effah, the headmaster of the school, left to assume the position of the district director of education for Daboase in the western region. During the five years that I worked with Mr. Effah, I had a very good personal and working relationship with him, and I learned a great deal from his statecraft. He helped me to realize my potential by giving me the necessary exposure, especially in public appearance and speech. In addition to my position as the housemaster and the PTA secretary, I was assigned the duty of the chairman of the PTA Implementation Committee. This committee was in charge of implementing the association's programs and activities in the school. These programs included the renovation of staff residences, staff welfare, student welfare, student academic progress, sports, and repairs to the lighting and sewerage systems in the school, among other things. I was also in charge of the lighting and sewage systems in the school, as well as being the deputy school imam (Muslim leader).

The multifarious functions that I performed in the school made me become a quasi member of the school administration. Mr. Effah instituted class and house meetings every other week at which students aired their views freely in the absence of any teachers. In addition, he instituted a crash program where students took biweekly tests in between the final examinations. All of this was geared toward academic improvement. The crash program was conducted by the examinations committee of the school. He ensured that teachers worked and students learned. All these programs were funded by the PTA, and the teachers were rewarded for the extra work on the crash program.

Furthermore, he instituted periodic durbar for the PTA executive committee and the student body without the presence of teachers; even the teachers' representative on the committee was not allowed to attend. At such gatherings, students were free to interact with their parents' representatives and freely expressed their views. According to Headmaster Alhaj Yakub A.B Abubakar's report on the Sixty-Third Speech and Prize-Giving Day of the school, all the programs that Mr. Effah initiated were still functional.

Mr. Y.K. Effah had his able assistants in the personalities of the late Mrs. Mary Akowua and Mrs. E.B. Ntiforo. Other members of the school administration and the senior house masters of the school, including Prince Amanfo, Kwabena Asumadu Yeboah, Ayub Morgan, and Muhammed K. Brako, all played prominent roles in the development of the school. Mention should be made of such teachers as the late Ahmed J.E. Adam, the late Emmanuel Asomani Ansong, Messrs G.K. Aidoo, Emmanuel Osei Mensah, Osei Agyeman, Ms. Angelina Ocran, Ms. Mary Donkor, the late Ms. Lucy Okyere, C.T. Mensah, Abdullah Mahmud Sam, the late Atta Sassu, and many more, all of whom worked tirelessly to assist Headmaster, Mr. Effah achieve his administration's objectives.

There was a good rapport between the headmaster and the members of staff, but he would not compromise on lackadaisical attitudes toward work. During breaks, he and his assistants would come to the staff common room to share ideas, tell jokes, and sip their beverages with the staff while going through the result sheets and the final report booklets to make sure those recalcitrant teachers were up to date.

What I admired most about Mr. Effah was his statistics in academic and sports progression at the staff meetings, which very often proved very successful. At his instance, the PTA renovated an abandoned dining hall to house some members of staff who had been ejected from a rented apartment building. I was actively involved in the renovation and happened to be a beneficiary of that project. By the end of his tenure as headmaster, he had brought the school in the limelight in academics, sports, and discipline—the hallmark of any good school administrator not only in Ashanti Region but Ghana as a whole.

As a sign of a good school administrator, Mr. Effah gave the boarding students leeway to buy food within a half-mile radius of the school up to seven o'clock in the evening without any punishment. It was an open secret that the meals offered to the boarding students were very inadequate because the schools had to struggle to get some of the necessary foodstuffs from suppliers. These food items were very often rationed to the institutions.

This was a period of Provisional National Defence Council government headed by Flt. Lt. Jerry John Rawlings in the mid-1980s when school administrators were experiencing difficult times in feeding boarding students. I will always remember him with his usual saying that "a small head is always better than a big tail." In fact, he left a landmark in the history of the school and will forever be remembered.

My Second Headmaster, I.K. Gyasi

The departure of Mr. Effah saw Mr. I.K. Gyasi taking over as the next headmaster of the school on September 3, 1990. He consolidated the good works of his predecessor with Mrs. E.B. Ntiforo, a hardworking and disciplinarian teacher as his able lieutenant. Both Mr. Gyasi and Mrs. Ntiforo happened to be my teachers when I was in the secondary school. In addition to maintaining the status quo, Mr. Gyasi added the school's infrastructure to his credit. He endeavored to see the completion of the administration block that had been abandoned for more than fifteen years.

He came to face an acute accommodation problem for the staff, so he suggested the construction of a staff residence to help alleviate the problem. The PTA agreed to his suggestion, and the Staff Housing Program was initiated. Being the chairman of the PTA Implementation Committee, I played a very vital role in the housing project. This brought additional responsibility on me, as I was made the secretary of the Building Committee formed at a general meeting of the association. I was deeply involved in the purchase of the building materials and the supervision of the project. The construction, which was started in July 1991, was completed in November 1993 and was able to house five teachers. It was a big relief to the accommodation situation in the school.

In December 1992, my friend Mr. Sam visited Ghana to attend the burial and final funeral rites of his late father, Mr. Mahmud Ahmed Sam (popularly called Bursar), who had died on December 18, 1992. The burial took place at Ekrawfo in the central region on December 23. He went back to Nigeria in January 1993 but returned about a year later and has since settled in Ghana.

At Ahmadiyya Secondary School, my wife and I had a small diversified farm of plantain, cocoyam, yam, cassava, maize, pepper, garden eggs, goats, and poultry. On June 29, 1993, as I was returning from school in the afternoon, I met my wife and son Akwasi with his hand bandaged. He had climbed our hen coop, and as he descended, one of his hands became trapped in between the wooden boards. One of his hands was fractured. I rushed him to the Komfo Anokye Teaching Hospital for medical treatment. After an x-ray, his hand was put in a cast for about six weeks, after which I sent him for traditional treatment at Aboabo, a neighborhood in Kumasi.

As the deputy school imam, I was almost always at the school's morning assembly either to give a sermon or to perform supervisory duties. On February 8, 1994, just after the day's sermon, one of the assistant school prefects made an emotional and inciting speech to the students in spite of the presence of some members of staff and announced that the students should boycott classes. He accused the school administration of cheating the students by increasing the cost of food for boarders. The government (Ghana Education Service) had announced increases in the food costs for all boarders in the country. The student council had met with the school administration to discuss the issue. The administration felt that the issue was over, but the student leaders, instigated by one of the assistants, claimed that they did not understand the headmaster's explanation, hence the call for the boycott. In his own words, "The explanation given to us by the school administration about the feeding money was not convincing enough." This situation threw the school into a state of pandemonium with some students becoming confused and not knowing what to do. The school had about 50 percent of the population who were day students as opposed to boarders.

The headmaster quickly arranged for an emergency staff meeting, and a resolution was made. The regional director of the Ghana Education Service was notified, as well as the Regional Police Command. The PTA executives also had an emergency meeting on the issue. The regional directorate of the Ghana Education Service met with the student body, and the Regional Student Representative Council also met with the student body later in the day. These meetings were all aimed at resolving the issue. The Regional Police Command dispatched some policemen to the school to protect life and property on the compound and to keep peace and order, especially during the nights. The students were sent home at the command of the metropolitan director of education.

On February 14, 1994, the school administration set up a disciplinary committee to investigate the circumstances leading to the student disturbances and to make recommendations to the school administration. I was made the secretary of the committee. The committee started its work on February 21, 1994, and submitted its report on March 2, 1994. The culprits were punished, and those not found to be connected were exonerated. The main architect of the plot was suspended till the end of his course but was permitted to write his final examination.

On July 22 I traveled to Anwhiaso in connection with the death of my aunt, Madam Amma Konadu, which occurred on the eighteenth of that month. She was eighty-three at the time of her death. I traveled with my wife, who was in the later stages of her pregnancy. On a Monday in July 1994, she gave birth to a baby boy, Ahmed Kwadwo Konadu Aboagye, named after my aunt who had just passed away. The next day I left for Kumasi to buy some necessities for the newborn and to bring some personal belongings of my wife. On Friday, July 27, we left Anwhiaso for Kumasi with our newborn. I left Kumasi for Anyanso on Friday, August 26, and on the following day, I was attacked by chicken pox. By the next day, my situation had worsened, with feverish conditions.

During the late evening, I could no longer bear the situation, so my late brother Zakariya accompanied me, and we walked a distance of about six miles while it was raining. We went to a clinic in Asiwa where I was treated and discharged. On November 26, 1994, I attended the final funeral rites of my late aunt Amma Konadu at Anwhiaso. On Saturday, December 22, I left Kumasi for Anyanso for the Christmas festivities with my family. We returned to Kumasi on December 30, and the next day I represented the school by attending the Junior Achievement workshop at the Ghana National Association of Teachers headquarters in Accra.

The one-week residential workshop, which started on Monday, January 2, ended on Friday, January 6, at the teachers' hall in Accra. I left Accra for Kumasi on January 9, 1995.

On Wednesday April 19, 1995, I visited my friend Mr. Sam at his school and observed that a heavy rainstorm had ripped the roofing off the school, T.I. Ahmadiyya J.S.S. "B." On June 29, I traveled with Alhaj Othman Yahya, then the PTA chairman, to Accra in search of a bus to purchase for the school, but that proved futile. On July 1, I attended a one-day Junior Achievement seminar at the teachers' hall in Accra with some Junior Achievement students of the school. On July 4 I traveled to Accra with the PTA chairman for the second time in search of a bus for the school. Again on July 11, I was attacked by fever and attended the stadium clinic. I was given seven days of sick leave. On Monday, July 17, we traveled to Accra for the third time for the school bus. Then two days later we finally bought a thirty-three-seater cargo Benz bus at the cost of 13 million (cedis). The PTA converted the cargo bus into a passenger bus at a further cost of about 10 Million (Cedis). Alhaj Othman Yahya, the chairman of PTA, handed over the keys of the completed bus to Mr. Gyasi, the headmaster of the school. It was a very colorful ceremony after the association's general meeting on the last Saturday of November 1995. Before the purchase of the bus, the school had only a wooden vehicle for both administrative and other duties.

On Friday, September 1, as I was traveling to New Edubiase, I was involved in a fatal accident when our minibus collided with another Benz bus on a road from Kumasi to Bekwai. At least five people lost their lives instantly whilst others were seriously injured. I had a minor injury and was treated and discharged from Okomfo Anokye Teaching Hospital. On September 13, I traveled to Atebubu with Adam Tuffour, one of my nephews who lived with me for his secondary school education, to enable him to attend an interview for admission to the Atebubu Teacher Training College. There, I met one of my college mates by the name of Gyimah. We returned to Kumasi the next day, after which I felt sick because of the aftermath of the motor traffic accident I had been involved in, the bad nature of the road to Atebubu, and the distance we'd had to walk from the town to the college compound. My condition worsened on Sunday, with shivering, vomiting, and sleeplessness. On Monday I attended the stadium clinic for medical treatment and was given one week of sick leave. Then, on September 26, I traveled to Accra to attend a Junior Achievement workshop at the teachers' hall. Before I boarded my bus to Accra, I accompanied Tuffour to the Kejetia bus station on Tuesday, October 10, on his way to Atebubu to start his college career.

As an Islamic studies teacher, realizing that there was no book on the subject, I took pains to publish a series of pamphlets to help my students. I started with the publication of the objective tests and later with the notes. The three series were on the historical development of Islam, the Koran and Hadith, and faith and jurisprudence (*tawhid* and *fiqh*). Even though there were few students taking the subject, I felt that it would enhance my teaching and also enable my students to read ahead and get more information on the subject.

In October 1996 the PTA decided to construct a girls' dormitory to ease the congestion at the makeshift girls' dormitory. The project was started in February 1997. As chairman of the PTA Implementation Committee, I was basically in charge of the project. I was deeply involved in the day-to-day purchasing of items, coordinating with the Building Committee members and the PTA executives, and overseeing the building experts hired to supervise the work.

I deem the year 1997 as my year of successes because of some significant achievements in my life. I attended three interviews during that year, and I was successful in all. First, I was invited for an examination and interview for admission to the University College of Education at Winneba on February 13, 1997. In April 1997 I received a letter of admission to the University College of Education at Winneba. Secondly, I was nominated by my headmaster for the Best Teacher Award for the second cycle schools in the Kumasi Metropolis. The interview took place on August 13, 1997, and I placed second in the contest. Furthermore, I attended a promotion interview for the position of principal superintendent for the Ghana Education Service. I was successful in this interview also.

On September 27 I handed over the proceeds of the Junior Achievement Program with a cash component of 160,000 (Cedis) to Mr. Ibrahim Acheampong. Three days later I handed over the work on the PTA girls' dormitory project to Mr. Amos Kusi with a cash component of 430,000 (Cedis).

By the beginning of September 1997, I knew very well that I was leaving the school for Winneba to continue my education. My major headache was where to accommodate my relatively large family, as I could not afford to rent an apartment to house them at the time. Mr. Gyasi did me a great favor. He agreed to let me keep my apartment until a makeshift accommodation was completed for me by the PTA. The understanding was that I would return to the school after the completion of my studies, even though this was not a usual practice. This kind gesture removed the burden of the accommodation problem from me, and I occupied that apartment during the two years of my studies. I must express my appreciation and that of my family to the headmaster and his administration for this great gesture.

CHAPTER 7

AT WINNEBA

Life at the University of Winneba

I left Kumasi on Thursday, September 25, 1997, to start my studies at the University of Education at Winneba for my degree program in Social Studies Education. The next day an orientation of the freshmen was conducted, and then on Thursday, October 2, registration for academic work began. The actual academic work started October 6. On October 8, I traveled to Kumasi for my September salary, paid my children's school fees, and bought some necessary items.

On October 24, I mailed the American Diversity Visa Lottery forms at the Winneba post office. The results were released in May 1998, and I was among the lucky winners. One afternoon as I was enjoying my siesta, a student knocked at my door. I opened the door and had the surprise of my life. I discovered I had won the American Diversity Visa Lottery. I had to complete some paperwork and return the completed forms to America.

During the first semester that year, I found the studies very tough because it was a new area of study for me. My contemporaries had completed their diplomas in social studies at the same institution some years back when it was a diploma-awarding specialist college. For them, it was a buildup of what they had learned some years before. However, I was determined to overcome my weaknesses by working extra hard. Fortunately, I joined a study group with some of the past students of the college. Our group included Mr. Matthias Edutuah, Mr. Amoako Minna, and Mrs. Adelaide Ferguson. Mr. Amoako Minna fell off the group as we moved along, but the rest of us remained committed to work together. At the end of our two-year course, we realized that the study group had been very beneficial to us. Mr. Edutuah obtained a first-class division, while Mrs. Fergusson and I obtained second-class upper division at the final examination.

Life at the University College of Education at Winneba was equally demanding. Water was a very big problem for the students on campus. On many occasions, especially during the dry seasons, the water would not run in the bathrooms or the outside standing taps. Though there were plastic reservoirs at the various residence halls, we constantly ran out of water. You either had to wake up early at dawn to fetch water from the lower level of the campus or wait till the daytime so that you could buy some water from a private reservoir in a nearby house. Because of the perennial water shortage, almost all the students had water containers to store water for cooking, drinking, washing, and bathing. Pit latrines had been constructed to complement the water closet toilets during the periods of water shortage.

Throughout my two years of study, my roommate was Samuel Oteng Ankomah, a nice student. I also met Nana Appiah-Kubi, an elderly student in his late fifties who also became my friend. He was a very passionate person who offered me advice on many occasions. We were living in the same neighborhood in Kumasi, and on many occasions, we traveled together to and from Kumasi during breaks and on some weekends. This friendship has grown ever since.

Many of the students, especially those taking degree courses, were either in their later forties or early fifties, but the diploma students were relatively younger. On the whole, many of the students had family responsibilities, so combining studies with family issues was very stressful for us. But at the same time, we felt the opportunity was an honor, because the completion of our studies would enhance our status. Some of these older students had been denied headship of secondary schools or other related positions in the Ghana Education Service because they did not possess university degrees, in spite of their competency and longer years of service.

The Genesis of My American Journey

In May 1998 I received a package from the American Diversity Visa Lottery organizers to attend an interview at the American Embassy in Accra-Ghana. I rushed to Tema to inform my friend and brother Mr. Kwadwo Antwi, alias Bob, about the interview. His immediate response was "Kwasi will help with your stay" without even consulting his younger brother who was in America. The other problem was with the finance pertaining to the medical examination, which was a prelude to the interview, visa processing, procurement, and finally the tickets if I were successful at the interview. I called Abena Amoah, alias Abena Addae, my wife's younger sister who was with her husband, Opanin Akwasi Addae, in America and told her of the situation. On July 21, 1998, our twenty-two-year marriage was registered at the Kumasi Metropolitan Assembly as a supporting document to our marriage. I started the processing of our passports at the Regional Immigration Office in Kumasi.

On Tuesday, October 6, 1998, I traveled to the American Embassy to reschedule our interview date, as our passports were not ready by then. Mr. R.O. Afum, a colleague and a beneficiary of the visa lottery, also attended an interview. On October 8 I traveled to Accra with my wife at the invitation of the Passport Office to make some clarifications pertaining to her change of name.

I talked with Abena, my wife's younger sister in America, about the visa expenses, and she promised to raise some funds to support us. She first sent some money for the medical examination. Though I was entitled to six visas, I could only raise money for my wife, two children, and myself due to financial constraints. I was scheduled for an interview on November 6, but because our passports were not ready by then, I traveled to the American Embassy to reschedule my appointment. The medical examination that was a prelude to the interview required our passports.

Initially, Abena sent me $2,000, the equivalent of 4.75 (cedis) million at that time, to cover the medical examination and interview. The cost of the medical examination was 175,000 (Cedis) per person. With our passports ready, we were left with an affidavit of support, and on November 25, 1998, we received one from Opanin Addae by courtesy of his white friend, Mr. Fred Seng. Armed with all our documents, on December 1, we presented ourselves for the interview at the American Embassy. The interview itself was nothing extraordinary if one possessed the required documents and qualifications. However, in my case, the bottleneck arose as a result of the change of name that I had made in 1975. It nearly stripped me of the opportunity. As the game of lottery has always been a winning or losing affair, one has to pay all the money involved—the cost of the interview, visa processing, and visa approval fees—before presenting yourself for the interview. The cost of all these processes per person was

$340 or its cedis equivalent. So when the interviewer requested further documents pertaining to my change of name, I realized that my approval was going to be delayed. On December 4 my friend Afum, who had also won the lottery, left Accra for America with his family.

The following week I presented all the necessary documents as scheduled and was given another appointment date. On the appointed date, I went to the embassy just to be told that the officer handling my case was out of the country, so I was rescheduled for another date. These appointments were usually between two weeks and one month apart. Thereafter, I went to the embassy so many times that I found myself in a state of dilemma and frustration, knowing how stressful going to the embassy was.

My frustration was not just losing the opportunity of going to America but rather how I would repay the millions of cedis that had already gone into that investment. I knew my monthly salary could not even cater for my immediate family, let alone pay such a huge debt. Sometimes I would see people weeping at the embassy when they were denied their visas. The weeping may not have just been caused by the denial of the visas, but by the reality that they would now have to somehow raise money to repay the loans they might have taken with the hope of repaying after they had arrived in America and began working for the almighty dollar.

In addition, there were hazards at the embassy, including standing in line for long hours amid hunger and thirst because you feared leaving your spot in the line. It was also an opportunity for the local residents who would stand in line beginning at dawn for prospective applicants for monetary compensation. My only hope and prayer was in Almighty God, the hope for the hopeless.

In spite of all these shuttles between Winneba, Accra, and Kumasi, I had an obligation to my lecturers and my studies. As all these frustrations and uncertainties were bothering my mind, I received an urgent telephone call from Kumasi. That was Thursday morning, February 25, 1999, and the accompanying message was that my son and his cousin had been detained at Asokwa Police Station over an issue with their employer. At the same time, I had been scheduled for an appointment at the American Embassy in Accra. That day coincided with the death of Otumfuo Opoku Ware II, the Asantehene (King of Ashanti) in Kumasi.

I left Winneba in the morning for Accra and the American Embassy, but I was rescheduled for another day. I then proceeded to Kumasi, reaching there at about nine o'clock at night. My late elder brother Zakariya was already in Kumasi. We then visited our children at the police station in the company of my wife and daughter Hanna and my late nephews Yaw and Asiedu. The police officer in charge called them to the counter, and when we saw them, we all began crying. However, we could not secure their release until the next day, which meant that they had spent three days in the police cell.

At this stage of my life, I was in a quadruple state of confusion, frustration, agony, and dilemma. I had not known the fate of my visa acquisition and all the millions of cedis that had gone into it. At this time, I was also preparing for the examination for the last semester of my course and also researching on my dissertation. My only hope of survival was in my Creator, Almighty God.

My brother and I decided to find a way to settle the case out of court to avoid further embarrassment from much publicity. At this juncture, I must express my appreciation and that of my family to the proprietor for the cooperation and understanding in all these trying periods for a very peaceful resolution. I must also be thankful to Mr. Rockson Harun Agyare, a friend and in-law for his assistance and support. My gratitude also goes to Nana Kwame Adarkwah, my former student and the assembly member for my village at the time, who took a leading role in the case even before I had heard of it. Mr. Rockson William Fosu, a friend, also deserves my gratitude for his assistance. I must also thank Nana Appiah-Kubi for his advice, counseling, and comfort at the university. Finally, my appreciation goes to all those who showed support and comfort in diverse ways during this uncomfortable period.

Notwithstanding the situation I found myself in, I tried as much as possible to subdue the frustration, pressure, and agony and went on with my normal routine. I attended lectures, researched for my dissertation, prepared for my impending examination, and traveled to the American Embassy on scheduled dates in addition to attending to family responsibilities. On March 15, 1999, as I was returning from the American Embassy in Accra to Winneba, someone stole my last twenty cedis while I was on a bus, and I had nothing on me to return to Winneba. Fortunately, I met one of the students from the university who loaned me five cedis to enable me return to campus.

On April 30, 1999, I received my promotion letter from the Central Regional Directorate of the GES to the grade of principal superintendent in the Ghana Education Service. On the afternoon of June 28 I was awakened from my siesta by a student who was there to tell me I had a telephone call at the reception area. At that time, mobile phones were not easily available in Ghana, so any student receiving a phone call had to rush to the hall's receptionist. When I took the phone, the caller was from the American Embassy and said I should proceed to the embassy immediately for an important interview. It was about three o'clock in the afternoon, so I told her that it would not be possible to reach Accra in good time considering the motor traffic congestion in the city. We then agreed to meet on the following day. There and then I realized that God had answered my prayer, and I was very optimistic of the issuance of the visa. I had an examination the following morning, so immediately after the examination, I traveled to Accra for the interview at the American Embassy. To my surprise and excitement, I was told to go ahead to pay the visa issuance fee of $240. It was like a bonanza. I then called Abena and her husband to inform them of the good news.

Thereafter, I traveled to Tema to inform my friend Mr. Kwadwo Antwi. The next morning I left Tema for Kumasi to inform my family that the stumbling block had been removed, and all was set for us to travel to America. It was very exciting news. Later in 2004 when I visited Ghana and went to my former school, the headmaster told me that a staff member from the American Embassy had visited the school to gather information about me. The staff left well convinced that I was actually a former member of the teaching staff. The headmaster even produced pictures I had taken with the staff and the executive members of the school's Parent-Teacher Association.

From Kumasi, I traveled to Anyanso to gather the final data for my dissertation. Two days later I returned to Winneba to join my colleagues at Asante Students Union in Winneba for an excursion to the Boti Falls on July 6, 1999. On July 8, I went to the embassy to pay for the visa issuance fee of $240 with money received from my benefactors. Then on July 15, I traveled to the embassy to collect the visas as scheduled. That ended the suspense and the eight months of shuttling to the embassy from Kumasi, Winneba, and Tema. The visas were a treasure to me, and I kept an eagle eye on them.

I wrote my last examination on Thursday, July 29, 1999, and on Saturday I left Winneba for Kumasi. On August 5 I traveled to Tema to receive $3,200 from Abena and her husband to cover our tickets. I then went to Winneba to consult my supervisor, Mr. Walter Blege, regarding my dissertation. Then on August 6, I returned to Kumasi via Accra. I purchased our tickets on August

13. Our flight was scheduled for August 24, 1999. On August 19, I traveled to Winneba to present my completed dissertation to the head of my department, Dr. Gyamfi Fenteng, and returned the following day.

I had previously informed my cousin Asare James, who was also in America, of my plight, and he assisted me with $500. I also contacted my cousin Adjei Amoako, a naval officer, regarding our problem with regard to immunization. Nurses in the public hospitals had embarked on a strike action to demand better conditions, so he helped us to get immunized at the military hospital in Accra.

On Sunday, August 22, we left Kumasi at night and reached Accra early Monday morning. We went to the military hospital for the immunization, and later in the evening, we left for Tema where we lodged with Mr. Kwadwo Antwi. On Tuesday August 24, 1999, at about three o'clock in the afternoon, we left Tema for Kotoka International Airport for the check-in. At the airport to see us off were Mr. Kwadwo Antwi, his younger brother David Oteng, and my elder cousin Hon. Kwadwo Kyei Frimpong.

CHAPTER 8

---•◆•---

THE JOURNEY TO
THE UNKNOWN

The Actual Journey

The initial stages of my life were at my village in Anyanso throughout my teenage years. As a day student at Ahmadiyya Secondary School in Kumasi, I lived in Asafo with my aunt, the late Abena Asubonteng. I later went back to my village as a professional elementary school teacher for four years. After my graduation from the University of Ghana I went back to my former school, Ahmadiyya Secondary School as a teacher from 1985 to 1997. I gained admission to Winneba College of Education for a degree in social studies education. It was at Winneba that I became a lucky beneficiary of the American Diversity Visa Lottery, which eventually made me migrate to the United States. This laudable program by the US government enables people from qualifying countries to settle in America as permanent residents. It is an opportunity for all people irrespective of social or economic status as long as basic education and work qualifications are met.

Our Ghana Airways flight was scheduled to take off at eight

o'clock on the evening on Tuesday, August 24, 1999, but was delayed till ten o'clock. It was as if we were living in a dreamland, as it was the first time we had boarded an airplane. Our plane stopped at Dakar in Senegal, West Africa, supposedly for fuel. We spent more than five hours there with no explanation. Eventually, we were informed that our plane could not continue the journey and the best alternative was to return to Accra. We reached Accra at dawn the next day and were taken to a hotel to rest until our next flight.

I called my brothers and friends to inform them of our plight. At about one o'clock the next afternoon we were picked up at our hotel and taken to the airport where we went through the immigration formalities and boarded a Ghana Airways flight for New York. Our anxiety and excitement were very high. I had a window seat, which afforded me the chance to have a bird's-eye view of the landscape. I hardly slept, as I was eager to observe any available thing that came my view. We had to stop at Dakar again for fuelling. We reached John F. Kennedy International Airport in New York at about one o'clock in the morning local time on the next day. As novices in air travel, we had to follow the other passengers, as we did not actually know where we were going.

In New York

Unlike Kotoka International Airport where the passengers have to descend from the airplane to the tarmac before going through immigration, New York was quite different. From the airplane, one has to pass through a movable jet bridge, a container-like hallway, and a very big concourse at the upper level of the building. One does not even see the tarmac. As we followed the other passengers, we walked for a distance before descending an escalator to the lower level where the immigration formalities were performed. The whole experience was amazing and unbelievable.

We were directed to form two lines, one for the American citizens and the other for noncitizens. With my briefcase firmly held in my armpit, I handed our visas and the supporting documents over to an immigration officer when she demanded them. We were then directed to an office and asked to wait. Thereafter, we were directed to another office where our passports were collected. Once there, they took our fingerprints and photographed each of us, and then we were made to sign some forms. We spent more than one hour at immigration.

Our passports were stamped with the inscription: "Temporary Evidence of Lawful Admission for Permanent Residence, Valid until August 2000. Employment Authorized." After the immigration formalities, we were directed to the baggage claim area where our three bags were waiting patiently for us. We were the last passengers to collect our luggage. Not knowing where to exit, I kept asking for directions, sometimes not hearing or understanding what exactly someone told us to go. The telephone system was very unfamiliar too.

When we got outside the building, it was late in the night and raining heavily. As we kept waiting, a taxi driver approached us and asked where we were going. I told him that we were going to the Greyhound bus station. He brought his car, and we loaded our bags in the trunk. We drove through New York City with lights of different shapes and colors illuminating everything. With very tall buildings and skyscrapers all along the route, I realized that we were very far away from home. The driver conversed with me throughout our journey, although sometimes I did not understand what he was really saying. We reached the bus station at about three o'clock in the morning on Thursday, August 25, 1999. The driver manipulated the meter, which was an unfamiliar device to me, and told me that the charge was two hundred dollars for the four of us. I made the payment, took our bags, and entered the adjacent building.

Later when I reached Chicago and told my story, I was informed that the driver had duped us. He should have charged me at most sixty dollars. Then I told myself that there are dishonest people everywhere. He probably took advantage of us because of my accent. In fact, I had been briefed that the bus fare from New York City to Chicago was eighty dollars per person, but for the taxi, I had no idea. When we entered the bus station, it was another surprise and quite different from our concept of a bus station in Ghana. It was a one-story building with a neatly kept terrazzo floor, complete with shops, restaurants, telephone booths, and very neat restrooms.

When I inquired about the Chicago-bound bus, I was told that it would leave at eight o'clock in the morning, which meant we had to wait for about five hours. We waited till daytime, and then I went for our tickets. I soon realized that we had run short of money because of the dishonest taxi driver and because when we returned from Dakar to Accra I had to use some money at the hotel for meals. Though I had some pound sterling on me there was no place to perform an exchange for me. I went to a money exchange shop, but they would not change for pound sterling. At the same time, we needed to buy some food to eat with some of the same money.

Fortunately, I met one Ghanaian who was working at the station, so I made my situation clear to him so he could assist us. He advised that I could buy three tickets and a one-half ticket for my daughter Aisha, who was smallish in nature. That's an advantage of being smallish. I handed $280 to the man for the tickets.

When he left, my son Kwadwo asked, "Daddy, what if the man does not come again?"

I then hurriedly followed him. He bought the tickets and then led us to a shop to buy some Coke, biscuits, and bread, the food very familiar to us. He then helped me make a call to Abena and her husband in Chicago so I could tell them we had reached New York City and were heading for Chicago. We were told that the journey was about eight hundred miles and would take more than fifteen hours.

At exactly eight o'clock in the morning, we boarded the bus bound for Chicago, which was half full. As the driver started the bus and was heading off, my wife remarked, "But the bus is not full." The comment marked a clear departure from what we were used to in Ghana. I then realized that we were in a different world altogether. It was still raining heavily as we drove through the streets of New York City among tall buildings, very wide streets, and large street lights. The journey took about eighteen hours with stops at designated terminals for some passengers to exit, while others boarded the bus. In some cases, drivers would change over. The driver would announce the time limit for reboarding. As we traveled along, I observed the wide dual highways with wide spaces between the lanes in the opposite directions, huge bridges, big rivers, and large tracts of forestland. Eventually, we reached Chicago at about one o'clock in the morning on Friday, August 26, 1999.

With the help of someone who dialed for me, I called Opanin Akwasi Addae and Abena to tell them that we had reached the Greyhound bus station in Chicago. Accompanied by his cousin Oppong, they came to pick us up at the station. At long last, the journey we had started on Tuesday ended on Friday. It was a momentous occasion, a family reunion, as all of us from the village of Anyanso, Ghana, had gathered at that material time in a foreign land. My wife and her younger sister were exceedingly happy, because they had not seen each other for about a decade. As were tired, Nana Addae suggested we cut the conversation and go to sleep.

CHAPTER 9

MY NEW HOME, CHICAGO

The End of the Journey at Last

The residence of our host was located at 4640 N. Sheridan Road, Chicago. In our ignorance, we brought from Ghana some fingers of plantain to let our host have the feeling of nostalgia. When we woke up the next morning, we discovered that Opanin Addae had purchased a box each of yams and plantains, as well as other food ingredients. Thus, our hope of surprising them with the few fingers of plantain was rendered useless.

During the next few days, Opanin Addae and his wife took us to meet some of their friends for the customary greetings and introduction. We visited some interesting places. Lake Michigan, which I had read about in my geography lessons in secondary school, was a short distance from our residence. We also saw the Sears Tower, now Willis Tower, which was the tallest building in the world at that time. I used the following week to write letters to friends and relatives at home to tell them about our experiences during our journey to America.

On Saturday, September 4, we traveled to Indianapolis,

Indiana, to attend an invitation extended to Opanin Akwasi Addae by his friend who lived there. On my off days, I used to go to downtown just to visit some interesting places and tourist centers, sometimes with my family. We watched huge bridges over the Chicago River, which is in the center of the city, and rode the elevated trains just for the exploration of the city. Sometimes I lost my bearings, which is part of the experience of being a stranger in such a big city.

During our second week in Chicago, we visited the office of the Social Security Administration to fill out our Social Security forms. Within that same period, Opanin Akwasi Addae, as he was then called, helped us to find a school for Agyeiwaa. She started high school at the Nicholas Senn High School on Tuesday, September 7, 1999. By September 10, all of us with the exception of my wife had received our Social Security cards, which enabled us to proceed with the process to obtain our state identity cards.

First Job

We received our permanent resident cards, otherwise known as green cards, on October 22, 1999, with the exception of my wife whose card was still unduly delayed.

With the assistance of Nana Akwasi Appiah, a friend of Opanin Addae and the Asantefuohene of Chicago at the time, I was able to secure a job with a parking company called Alright Parking at the Wabash and Balbo facility. It is very common for new immigrants, professionals and nonprofessionals alike, to take some rough jobs before landing on a good job. In most cases, your work may not be necessarily linked to your profession or your certificate. In order to continue with your previous profession or course of study, you must attend an American institution. You can also switch to another profession by attending an institution.

Before your enrollment in any institution, your certificate would be evaluated by an independent evaluation board.

After my last interview when I got the green light to start work the next Monday, Nana Akwasi Appiah showed me a workshop where I could go to take my measurement for a uniform. He further said to me, "If you have blue pants and a white shirt, you could come to work with it until your uniform is ready." The mention of blue pants surprised me. In my moment of soliloquy, I saw some of the workers wearing white shirts and blue trousers. I then realized that Nana was making reference to trousers and not the pants that I was familiar with.

In another development, I went to a coffee shop for some coffee after a night of work. When it was my turn, the lady gave me a cup of coffee and sugar. She asked me if I needed cream. I answered no. I then asked for milk. The lady was staring at me in bewilderment. I quickly realized that we did not understand each other. As there was a long line of customers behind me, I took my black coffee away. Thereafter, I began familiarizing myself with some American terminology: washroom/restroom/bathroom for toilet, elevator for lift, Wite-Out for correction fluid, resume for curriculum vitae (CV), soccer for football, period for full stop, county for district, trunk for boot, and many more. Incidentally, when I was in Leeds, England, in 2010 while on my way to Ghana, I went to a shop and asked a gentleman to show me the restroom. This gentleman looked at me in amazement until I changed my term to toilet before he showed me.

My son Kwadwo started working at a parking facility in the nearby town of Evanston on September 18. He obtained this job with the help of Mr. Andy Aninagyei, who was then the manager at that location.

In an attempt to locate my fellow worshipers, the Ahmadiyya Muslim Community, I called the Ahmadiyya headquarters in

Ghana and got the address of the Mission. One Friday, I asked Opanin Addae to take me to the Ahmadiyya Muslim Mission, which is located at 2134 W. Van Buren Street. I introduced myself to the congregation. After worshipping there for some time, I learned about another location of the Mission called Al Sadique Mosque at 4448 S. Wabash Avenue on the south side of Chicago. This is where I have been worshiping ever since. Al Sadique Mosque was the first Ahmadiyya Mosque built in the United States in July 1922, though it has been rebuilt at the same location. Later, I met some of my former students there, and we have become closely related ever since.

By the time we arrived in Chicago, I was indebted to the tune of about $8,000, as well as about 1 million (Cedis) in the local currency. At this juncture, I must express our heartfelt gratitude to Nana Akwasi Addae and his wife, Obapanin Abena Addae, for their financial assistance and moral support. Abena's commitment to assist us marked a laudable reciprocity of the assistance she received from us when she was an apprentice seamstress at Kumasi in the mid-1980s. At the same time, my lifelong friend Mr. Kwame Danso also deserves some gratitude for his financial support.

We stayed with Opanin Addae and his family until March 31, 2000, when we moved to occupy our own residence just a short distance from theirs. He helped us to acquire a residence in an apartment building at 810 W. Grace Street. We lived in a two-bedroom apartment on the fifth floor on a twenty-seven-floor apartment building. Later, we moved to a three-bedroom apartment on the twenty-sixth floor in the same twenty-seven-floor building when our family size increased.

In recognition of my services to the PTA and the school in general, the association offered me an honorarium of 3 million (Cedis). I am happy to express my gratitude to the association. Now that we were in America, my next area of concern was how to relocate my children in Ghana and settle the debts I owed. After consulting with my friend Mr. Sam, my children moved to live with him for about four months until I was able to rent an apartment for them. Then my son Kwadwo and I started to settle our debts on monthly payments, as my wife was not working at that time. On March 31, 2000, I left the employment of Alright Parking, and on April 17, I started to work with Prospect Airport Services at the O'Hare International Airport, one of the busiest airports in the world. I worked as a passenger service agent. Before I started work, I was required to undergo a physical examination and present the report to management. Employees were expected to have necessary vaccination, and where deficient, you would take the necessary medications for treatment.

I worked at the airport for four years before returning to Ghana for a two-month holiday. I rejoined the company on my return from Ghana.

Substitute Teaching

I applied to be a day-to-day substitute teacher with the Chicago Public Schools as a part-time job. My first day of work was on February 27, 2001. What I realized at my substitute teaching assignments was that the school system was far different from Ghana's with respect to discipline, equipment, facilities, and personnel. As we could not compare our facilities and resources to theirs, discipline was and is a big problem in some US public schools when compared to what exists in Ghana. One must have a very big stomach to deal with anything within the six hours that one will be with the students, especially as a substitute teacher, popularly shortened to the word *sub*.

A good friend of mine, Yaw Obeng Adu-Asare, a retired high school mathematics teacher in New York City, once said, "If you have a bad temper, you should leave it at home before entering the school premises."

This friend was among those of us who trekked from Anyanso to attend the middle school at Asiwa. He left Asiwa middle school after one year and continued in elementary school in Konongo, an urban town. After his elementary school education, he learned a trade as an auto electrician.

According to him, in the early 1970s, he left Ghana through some hazardous journeys to Mali and Senegal in West Africa. He then lived in Dakar (Senegal) for about a year where he learned the French language. By God's grace, he had an opportunity to travel to Brussels where he got a job with his skills as an auto electrician, coupled with his ability to communicate in French. This enabled him to fund his college education. He later transferred to the United States and lived in California. With hard work and tenacity of purpose, he enrolled in a seminary where he obtained a master's degree in divinity. In 1999 he moved to New York City and started courses in mathematics at Staten Island College where he obtained his master's degree in mathematics. Yaw Obeng Adu-Asare is now a retired certified New York State mathematics teacher.

In both elementary and high schools, teachers have to accompany their students to the playground and supervise them, even in the use of the restroom. As a substitute, you will indicate your preparedness to work the following day by calling the substitute center automated system. If there is a vacancy the next morning, the substitute center will call you and request you to go to whatever school needs a substitute. You may go to a classroom or any other place available. If you happen to be assigned to a well-disciplined school, you would like the job. On the other hand, if you were assigned to a poorly disciplined school, the six hours of duty would feel like twenty-four hours.

As soon as the students saw you, one of them would shout to the others, "We get a sub." The problem would begin from there. Some would sarcastically ask, "You have an accent. Do you come from Africa or Jamaica?" Sometimes, those of us who did not pass through the American school system find it hard to comprehend the behavioral pattern of some students.

A chaotic classroom situation is aptly described by James P. Comer in his book *Maggie's American Dream*:

> At Baldwin three of the fourteen classrooms were totally out of control. Eight were on the edge and could have fallen apart at any moment. Only the three classrooms with veteran teachers were functioning adequately. I went into one of the classrooms and could not believe my eyes and ears. There were a couple of eight-year-olds chasing each other around the room. Two were standing on tables screaming across the room, imitating something they had seen on television. Other children were whining and crying, "Teacher, teacher." One child was walking aimlessly around the room opening and closing cabinet drawers, dumping paint brushes, pounding erasers and doing whatever else came to his mind with the next thing he encountered. The noise was incredible. Anxious children were sucking their thumbs in an effort to find comfort. The shaken teacher called for order. The children ignored her. I called for order in my most firm and assertive way. They hesitated a second and then ignored me. That had never happened to me before with children. Mrs. Brown, assistant

to the Principal for administration, arrived. She was a black woman, a senior teacher, and one of the three people in the project who had been in the school the year before. She knew the children and their parents, and she was able to get them to quiet down. But she couldn't stay there and teach. I retreated to the hallway. One of the children who had been crying followed me out of the door. I noticed that he was behind me as I started the stairs. He was scared and held out to his arms. I instinctively embraced him to give comfort, but also to receive it. I was almost frightened as he was. As he sobbed, his small body trembled against mine. I thought to myself, "Kid, what are we doing to you?" One part of me said, "What am I doing here?" and wanted to run. The other part of me said, "You want to make a difference and this is your chance."

In an undisciplined school, the teachers are subjected to many problems by the children. In the classroom, some students will be walking or running aimlessly, while others will be throwing objects around. The big students would be bullying the smaller ones. Those who want to concentrate on their studies would be disturbed by others. The teacher would become disturbed because the students would flout instructions or appeals for calm. In such a situation, the substitute teacher would have to buzz security who would come for the affected students and escort them to the office. After some time, the students would be released from the office back to the classroom. Substitute teachers are mostly not respected in undisciplined schools, because some of the children have the notion that subs do not know their parents. At one particular school where I substituted, I drove nearly half of the students from the classroom because the situation became unbearable.

Chicago Experience

In April 26th, 2001 I accompanied my wife to New York to board a Ghana Airways flight to Accra, Ghana. Upon reaching La Guardia Airport, we could not find one of her pieces of luggage. Tracing the lost baggage caused such an undue delay that she eventually missed her flight to Accra. She was rescheduled for Thursday, May 3, 2001, so we had to stay with Ibrahim Acheampong, a colleague at Ahmadiyya Secondary School, in the Bronx, New York for almost one week. She stayed in Ghana for six months learning hair braiding. She returned from Ghana on Tuesday, October 8, 2001, and I met her at Dulles Airport in Washington, DC.

On April 4, 2002, my first child, Hanna Aboagye, and her husband, Prince Kwasi Agyare, performed a wedding ceremony in Kumasi, Ghana. Some of my colleagues and friends at T.I. AMASS attended the event. At this juncture, I would like to express my heartfelt appreciation to my friend Alhaj Othman Yahya for providing his car for the wedding ride. Earlier on, he had traveled to Anyanso for the engagement ceremony, even without my knowledge. I must also thank my friends William Rockson Fosu, then accountant of the school; Amissah John, the school electrician; and Juliana, the school matron, who all traveled to Anyanso for the engagement, as well as the wedding event, all unknown to me. My heartfelt appreciation goes to my best friend Mr. Sam, who doubled as the guardian of my children, as well as G.K. Aidoo, Osei Mensah, Mrs. E.B. Ntiforo, and Nana Appiah Kubi. They all proved to me that, though out of sight, my relationship with them was still as strong as ever before.

I arrived in America at the tail end of President Bill Clinton's administration in 1999. George Bush became the next president from 2000 to 2008. The 2008 election was a very crucial one. The young Senator Barack Obama, the first African American to become a presidential candidate of a major political party, ran for the Democratic Party against Sen. John McCain of the Republican Party. People were glued to their televisions for the three debates of the candidates.

On Election Day, November 4, 2008, I sat in the comfort of my home watching the television and waiting for the final results to be announced. At about eleven o'clock at night, central time, after the western polls had officially closed, Obama, along with his running mate Joe Biden, had won in a convincing fashion. He won 364 electoral votes as against McCain's 174 votes; 270 electoral votes are required to win.

As I watched the event on the television at Chicago's Grant Park, I could see people, especially blacks, shedding tears of joy and disbelief, including Rev. Jesse Jackson, a civil rights advocate. John McCain gave a congratulatory concession speech from his headquarters in Phoenix, Arizona. Just before midnight, the party really got going in Grant Park. In front of more than 250,000 supporters, the new president-elect took the stage to give his speech. It was a monumental moment to watch him speak, with many attendees shedding tears of excitement and amazement.

Barack Obama II was born on August 4, 1961. As a junior US Senator from Illinois, he led the Democratic Party to victory. Obama is the forty-fourth president of the United States and the first African American to be nominated and elected as president of the United States. A graduate of Columbia University and Harvard Law School, where he served as president of the Harvard Law Review, Obama worked as a community organizer and practiced as a civil rights attorney before serving three terms in the Illinois Senate from 1997 to 2004. He taught constitutional law at the

University of Chicago Law School from 1992 to 2004. Following an unsuccessful bid for a seat in the US House of Representatives in 2000, he announced his campaign for US Senate in January 2003, and he won that race in November 2004. He was the keynote speaker at the Democratic National Convention in July 2004, which brought him to national prominence. In November 2008 he defeated Mitt Romney to secure a second term as president of the United States. (source: the Historic Inauguration in Photography, January 20, 2009)

Chicago's rich and diverse culture is celebrated across the city and throughout the year. Cultural festivals attract young and old to neighborhoods founded by the generation of immigrants who built their homes there. The city is home to twenty-six ethnic groups, and Chicagoans collectively speak more than one hundred languages. Chicago is home to more than fifty skyscrapers and a lot more superstructures, bascule bridges, and historic sites, with Chicago River running through the city. Chicago has more than five hundred recreational parks of varying sizes, as well as twenty-nine miles of lakefront. Chicago has seventy-seven distinct neighborhood communities, some of which are worth mentioning. (source: *Newcomer's Handbook*)

On May 23, 2009, my entire family and Obaapanin Abena Addae, attended an engagement ceremony of my son Sadik Bosompem Aboagye Jr. to Linda Obeng at South Holland, Illinois. Their wedding took place in Chicago on June 27 of the same year. Another engagement ceremony was performed between my daughter Aisha Agyeiwaa Aboagye and Henry Kwame Darko on August 22. Unfortunately, Nana Akwasi Addae was in Ghana. In both engagement ceremonies, Nana Kwame Frimpong was the master of ceremonies. In attendance at all these ceremonies were Nana Addae Baffour, Asantefuohene, Ohemaa Abena Amponsah, Asantefuohemaa; and Nana Akwasi Appiah, ex-Asantefuohene, as well as some elders and executive members of Asanteman Association. At this juncture, I should express my gratitude and that of my family to all those who participated in all the ceremonies.

I became a naturalized US citizen at a swearing in ceremony on Monday, October 26, 2009. At that ceremony, more than sixty people from more than forty countries across the world were sworn in by a Judge.

On May 9, 2010, my family and the family of Nana Akwasi Addae attended the graduation ceremony of my daughter, Aisha Agyeiwaa Aboagye (Aisha Aboagye Darko), at Aurora University in Aurora, Illinois. Her husband, Henry Kwame Darko, was also in attendance. Aisha earned her second bachelor's degree in 2010. The following week, on May 16, my son Sadik Bosompem Aboagye Jr. graduated from Trinity International University in Deerfield, Illinois. My family was joined by Mr. and Mrs. Dadzie, Sadik's in-laws, and, of course, Linda Obeng Aboagye his wife. My son-in-law Henry Kwame Darko was also in attendance. Sadik obtained his master's degree. Sera Aboagye and Akwasi Aboagye obtained their bachelor's degrees in 2013, while Osam Aboagye also graduated in 2014, all in various disciplines.

I, on the right, late Osei in the middle and late Afoakwa on the left – December 12th, 1969

Returning from lectures at Bagabaga teacher
Training College, Tamale, 1972

At Bagabaga - 1972

A teacher at Anyanso, my village, 1975

My wife, Mariam Aboagye in 1978 at Anyanso

At the University of Ghana – Lgon, Accra, October 1980

Late Mr. Y.K. Effah, headmaster receiving award
from the late Alhaj V.A. Essaka, Chairman
of PTA AMASS, February 26, 1990

At T.I. AMASS, Kumasi 1994 with children after the festival prayers. From right – front row, Osam Aboagye, Sera Aboagye, Akwasi Aboagye, Aisha Aboagye. Back row: From right, Hanna Aboagye, I and Sadik Aboagye

Reading minutes at a PTA general meeting,
T.I. AMASS, November 1994.

With children, Hanna in the middle and Sadik on
the right at Barekese Dam, October 1994

Giving a demonstration lesson at a Junior Achievement
workshop at the Teacher's Hall, Accra, January 4th. 1995

Receiving an award from the late Edward Salia,
then minister for Education at the Speech and
Prize Giving Day at AMASS, June 1995

At the opening of Manhyia Palace Museum, August 20th. 1995

Trying my hands on the PTA bus purchased
for the School, November 1995

At AMASS, 1996

My wife, Mariam Aboagye, plucking some garden
eggs from our farm at AMASS, August 1996

Late brother, Adjei Zakariyya

Inspecting work on the PTA girl's
dormitory project, May 4th. 1997

Giving a speech at the Re-Launching of
the school magazine, June 1997

At a snack bar operated by the AMASS Junior
Achievement Program, July 1997

At the matriculation ceremony, University
of Winneba, November 21, 1998

At the Elmina castle, December 12, 1998

At the Cape Coast castle, December 12, 1998

At the Kakum National Park, December 12, 1998

The Aboagye family, August 1999 before emigrating to
the United States. Front row: From right; Osam Aboagye,
Konadu Aboagye and Akwasi Aboagye. Rear row; From
right-Hanna Aboagye, Sera Aboagye, Sadik Aboagye Jr.,
Aisha Aboagye, Wife Mariam Aboagye and I at extreme left

Sadik and Aisha on vacation in Kumasi, March 2003 with their siblings; from right; Hanna, Akwasi, Osam, Aisha, Konadu, Sadik and Sera.

Late brother Adjei Zakariyya

Wife, Mrs. Mariam Aboagye

With wife Mariam in Kumasi on March 30th.
2004 in connection with the mother's funeral

Mariam Aboagye at Marriott Hotel for Black Tie event, 2004

The Aboagye family at Sadik's wedding, June 27, 2009. From left; Aboagye Konadu, I, Aisha Aboagye, Sadik Aboagye, Linda Aboagye, Sera Aboagye, Mariam Aboagye, Akwasi Aboagye and Osam Aboagye.

With wife, Mariam at Ghanafest, Chicago, July 2010

At Marriott Hotel for Black Tie event, 2004

At downtown Leeds, England, October 18, 2010

Relaxing during vacation in Ghana, November, 2010

After a wedding reception in Tema, Ghana, 2010

With cousins, late Elizabeth Kyei on right and late Mary Kyei on the left, Accra, Ghana, October 28, 2010

At Asokore T.I. AmASS, November 2010

CHAPTER 10

———•◆•———

BACK TO THE HOMELAND

My First Journey to Ghana

On Tuesday November 11, 2003, my family received the bad news of the death of Madam Akosua Ataa, alias Alice Adoma, my mother-in-law. She had been at the Emena Hospital in Kumasi. As Nana Addae and I married two sisters, we had a meeting at Nana Akwasi Addae's residence after hearing about the death of our mother-in-law. We decided that time was not on our side to attend the burial, so burial should take place, but the final funeral rites should be scheduled for the year 2004, as it was nearing the Christmas festivities. This decision was communicated to the family in Ghana. Later, the final funeral rite was scheduled for Saturday, April 3, 2004.

On March 11, 2004, Nana Akwasi Addae left Chicago for Ghana, and then on Tuesday, March 23, Abena Addae boarded a KLM flight for Ghana. My wife and I boarded a British Airways flight to Ghana the same day, all in connection with the final funeral rites of our beloved Maame Akosua Ataa. This was my first visit to Ghana for almost five years since my departure from Ghana to America on August 26, 1999.

We reached Kotoka International Airport in Accra, Ghana, at 6:50 p.m. the next day. My first experience was the hot air that greeted us as soon as we got down from the airplane. So I asked myself in disbelief whether the weather conditions had been the same when we lived in Ghana. The situation worsened when we entered the immigration room for the immigration formalities. The oven-like heat was unbearable. We were told that the air-conditioning had broken down, and there was no fan to mitigate the intensity of the heat. However, we were glad that we had reached our homeland.

When we completed the departure formalities and got outside, we found that Nana Akwasi Addae, Nana Akwasi Appiah, and Mr. Kwadwo Antwi had been patiently waiting for us. We gladly embraced one another and conversed for some time before leaving for home with Mr. Kwadwo Antwi. Because Abena Addae had not arrived, Nana Addae had to wait for her. We spent the night in Tema but sent a message to Kumasi that by the grace of the Almighty God, we had safely arrived in Ghana.

The remaining hours of the night became too long for us, as we were eager to see our children in Kumasi. The next day we went to town to greet some relatives and friends before leaving for Kumasi in the afternoon with the state transport bus. We left Tema at two o'clock in the afternoon and arrived in Kumasi at about eight o'clock that evening. At the transport terminal waiting for us were my daughter Hanna Aboagye and my brother-in-law Appiah Emmanuel. My friends, Mr. Sam and Mr. Rockson William Fosu, had been waiting for us since six o'clock but left for home. Upon reaching the terminal, Hanna called Mr. Sam to tell him of our arrival. In a few minutes, he arrived at the terminal. The joy of seeing each other after almost five years was beyond imagination. With the five of us and our four big bags, it became necessary to hire a taxi from the terminal to our house.

My younger children were waiting patiently for us. Finally, we reached home at about nine o'clock at night. The scene at the house was much of exhilaration—a family reunion. We conversed almost the whole night, and I realized that I had missed a very good component of family life.

My children had also missed the parental affection of a caring father for a long time. Early the next morning I called my friend Mr. Rockson and informed him of our arrival. He visited us at the house before going to work.

At My Village, Anyanso

Time was not on our side, as we had barely one week for the celebration of the final funeral rites of my late mother-in-law. As custom demanded, we had to go to the village to greet the people and express our gratitude to those who helped in the burial of our late mother and to meet the relatives to discuss the necessary preparations for the final funeral celebration. At Tema, we agreed that we would go to Anyanso at the same time, so we decided to meet Nana Addae and Abena at Konongo. At about three o'clock in the afternoon on Friday, March 26, 2004, we met them at Konongo. As we had no means of transport, Mr. Sam offered us a ride to Konongo to join them en route to Anyanso. Honestly speaking, our stay in Ghana and, for that matter, in Kumasi was made very convenient and smooth with the help of Mr. Sam who offered his services throughout our stay. It is said, a friend in need is a friend indeed. We really owe him a debt of gratitude. We must also not forget Mr. Rockson who performed similar functions to ease our transportation problems.

Upon reaching our village, the first thing we did was visit the graveyard of our late mother. Thereafter, we went to the house of the head of the family of the deceased for the customary exchange of greetings. Friends and relatives poured in to extend warm greetings, which is common in a village community. Some embraced us, while others shook hands with us. I barely slept that night as I chatted with friends who wanted to hear more news from abroad.

The next morning we had to visit almost every home to greet everyone and express our gratitude for their services to the deceased. First we went to the chief's palace to greet him and his elders and to express our appreciation for their assistance in the burial process. I had lived in Anyanso through most of my life, and in order not to incur the displeasure of any individual or family, I made sure that we went to every available house. That is the village life.

On the next Monday my wife and I left for Kumasi to prepare for the great occasion. Nana Addae and his wife remained at Anyanso but kept frequenting Kumasi to purchase the necessary items for the funeral celebration. From Monday through Thursday, I ensured that I visited all my friends, colleagues, and relatives in Kumasi. My most frequent spot was at T.I. AMASS, my former workplace where most of my colleagues were based, especially those I could not visit in their homes.

On Thursday, April 1, 2004, my wife joined Nana Addae and his wife to go to Anyanso, and the next day I followed. Before I went, I had to make sure that all the necessary ingredients for the funeral had been conveyed to Anyanso. As usual, my friend Mr. Sam drove me to Anyanso after the Friday prayer. We left Kumasi at about three o'clock in the afternoon and reached Anyanso at four thirty. The wake was scheduled for the night, as we were watching the video coverage of the burial activities. Mr. Sam attended the burial activities during our absence. Saturday and Sunday were the days for the final funeral rite of our late mother. Mr. Sam Abdullah and Mr. Rockson Fosu attended the funeral on Saturday, and on Sunday Mrs. E.B. Ntiforo, my former assistant headmaster, and Miss Mercy Woode, a former colleague, attended the funeral with Mr. Sam again. On my own behalf and on the behalf of my family and the entire bereaved family, I wish to express my appreciation to them all for mourning with us.

I left Anyanso with my wife on Wednesday, April 7, but my wife returned the next Monday. That same day I was attacked by fever and had to attend the Atonso-Agogo Hospital where I was treated and discharged. A week later I traveled to Tema to pick up some items we had shipped to Ghana. I waited till Saturday, but I was not able to pick up the goods and had to return to Kumasi. About ten days later I was notified that I could secure the items. As expected from someone returning home from being abroad, I had to give some gifts to friends, colleagues, and relatives. Though one cannot satisfy everybody, one must be cautious with certain group of people.

I spent most of my time with my family in Kumasi and made periodic visits to my hometown. I returned to the United States on May 23, but my wife spent more time in Ghana and returned to Chicago on August 25. Upon my return from Ghana, I had to reapply at my former place of work at O'Hare International Airport and still continued with the substitute teaching. After working at the airport for almost two years, I decided to leave the job. I continued with the substitute teaching for some time while looking for permanent employment.

CHAPTER 11

------·•◆•·------

LIFE AS A CHAUFFEUR

Qualifications of a Chicago Chauffeur

Substitute teaching is not a permanent job, because when schools aren't in session, you have no work. Brenneman Elementary School employed me continuously for three months, but when schools let out for the summer, I had to look for a more permanent job. So in August 2006, I decided to drive a taxi, which I felt was the best alternative open to me.

I went to Harold Washington College to inquire about it. Before I could register for the class, I had to pass a test in language proficiency in writing and speaking. The basic qualification is that the candidate must be twenty-one years or older, have a valid US driver's license, and have a good driving record. The same things are required for livery and limousine drivers. I had to pay $275 for the two-week class. On the first day of the class, we had to introduce ourselves. Out of the twenty-five students in the class, twelve had bachelor's degree in various disciplines of study. There were Africans, Europeans, and Asians in the class.

As a qualified chauffeur, I had the chance to talk to the

owner of a mechanic shop where I used to service my vehicle. This Indian told me that he was a medical practitioner in India but could not get a license to practice medicine when he came to America, in spite of the many interviews that he attended. He ended up as a chauffeur, driving a limousine. He said at one point he owned seven limousines but later decided to sell all of them to establish the mechanic workshop. This is an example of the plight of some immigrant professionals who become frustrated and underemployed in developed countries. However, this man told me that two of his children who had been educated in Chicago had become medical doctors practicing in Chicago. With the exception of some immigrant professionals who are recruited by companies and institutions and have specialized visas, the majority of professionals from developing countries are more likely to do some rough jobs before landing on a good job later.

In his book *I'm Not a Crazy Cabbie*, Chuck Okofor said:

> They have come to America from every corner of the world in pursuit of a better life for themselves and their families. Dozens of countries of the world are represented in the Chicago cabbies community. Of course, there are native born Americans, but it is worthy of note that over 90% of cabbies are first generation immigrants. They are usually well-educated, in such fields as lawyers, engineers, bankers, business administrators, teachers but as first generation immigrants, they may be inhibited by their accent which sometimes makes them unable to communicate effectively with the average American. Secondly, some of them who obtained their degrees from universities

in their home countries have degrees that are not highly regarded by employers in America.

Okafor is a retired cab driver and holds a master's degree in Curriculum Development from his home country of Nigeria.
(source: Ibid, page 38)

The two-week comprehensive Public Chauffeur Training Program I registered for had three main components: the rules and regulations of the taxi industry, the geography and navigation of the City of Chicago and the suburbs, and customer service skills. The course was designed to prepare participants to become public chauffeurs in Chicago. The candidate must pass the examination conducted at the end of the course and pass the Chauffeur Licensing Examination conducted by the Business Affairs and Consumer Protection (BACP), which covered the areas of study.

Rules and Regulations of the Taxi Industry

The rules and regulations of the taxi industry in the City of Chicago are contained in a forty-six-page document that covers many areas of the industry. These rules and regulations include, but are not limited to, the following: the requirements for the Chauffeurs Training Courses, license renewals, chauffeur conduct, change of address, vehicles fit for taxis, leased vehicles, fares, passengers, operations at the airports, taxi access programs and wheelchair-accessible vehicles (WAV) and above all, penalties for any violation of the rules. A new chauffeur must pass a physical test conducted by a licensed physician in Illinois, a drug test for chemical detection of any controlled substance or cannabis, and vision and hearing tests. A prospective chauffeur must also be fingerprinted. The candidate will have to provide a Motor Vehicle Record (MVR) obtained from the Office of the Secretary of State as well as any criminal record. The same procedure affects even those in the system who must renew their licenses each year, no matter how long the individual has driven a taxi. The most common rules include discourtesy to passengers, assault and abusive language and behavior, reckless driving, operating under the influence of drugs or alcohol, and driving an unclean vehicle both inside and outside. Only a licensed chauffeur is permitted to operate a taxicab, and the lessee should be the only operator of the taxicab and have his chauffeur license clearly displayed in the taxi.

The public chauffeur must return to his affiliation any recovered article in his taxi within twenty-four hours. Equipment in the taxi must include a credit card processor for accepting credit card payments, a shield or security camera for the safety of the driver, two-way radio system for communication with the dispatch operator, and an information sheet displaying the charge for riding. The responsibilities of the driver and the passenger should also be displayed. Each taxi should also contain the phone number for complaints as well as compliments to BACP. Violation of any of these rules and regulations is punishable either by the payment of fines or an order to go back to school for remedial classes. The department deserves the right to revoke any chauffeur's license for repeated violations and also for giving false statements.

The second component of the program is the geography and navigation of the City of Chicago. The driver must have a good geographical knowledge of the city and its suburbs or must have reference material readily available to transport the passenger to his destination. In some instances, some drivers use Global Positioning System (GPS). The geographical locations drivers need to be familiar with include but are not limited to hospitals, government office buildings, museums, monuments, hotels, institutions of higher learning, theaters, places of general interest, skyscrapers and superstructures, and the highway system. The driver must use the most direct route from one location to another unless the passenger has an alternative or preferred route. The streets of Chicago are in the form of a grid system; one has to be familiar with the cardinal streets. Madison Street divides the city into north and south, while State Street divides the city into east and west. Each count of eight hundred equals one mile. This helps drivers and other road users to navigate through the city with some ease.

The third part of the program covers the customer service and public relations aspect. As the taxi business is considered as the gateway to the city, the department does not compromise on attitudinal deficiencies of chauffeurs. Consequently, drivers are expected to display professionalism to passengers, including good appearance, a clean taxi, courteous attitude, willingness to assist passengers with their luggage, and generally being polite, because you never know who you are picking up. Payments with credit cards must be accepted, but no extra fee can be charged. There should also be no charge for luggage. Children younger than twelve and adults older than sixty-five are not charged as extra passengers. (Source: City of Chicago; Department of Business Affairs and Consumer Protection website)

Upon completion of my course, I passed the course examination, but when I took the department examination, I was among those who failed for lack of adequate knowledge of the geography of the city. I had to reregister for the class and pay the required fees. I took the city examination for the second time and was successful. Thereafter, I obtained my professional chauffeur's license. Armed with my chauffeur's license, I began driving in earnest. I began driving for American United Taxi Association but later joined the Gold Coast Taxi Association, for which I have been driving ever since.

Chicago has a lot of taxi associations with varying numerical strengths. Among the various associations is the Gold Coast Taxi Association, a wholly Ghanaian association with a Ghanaian identity. It's the only taxi association owned by the nationals of a particular country. It is owned by some Ghanaian medallion owners with the able manager John Henry Assabill. He is a medallion owner himself and drives his own taxi, so he ensures that the interests of the members of the association are cared for. Through his untiring efforts, a number of Ghanaians have acquired their own costly medallions.

At the celebration for the fifty-sixth anniversary of Ghana's independence, the guest speaker was Mr. Mike Rosenstein, president of Transit Funding. He said the following about John Henry Assabill: "I met John Henry many years ago when he brought into my office a customer who wanted to buy a medallion but had no money for a down payment. Not only did we do this one but we have financed 26 other medallions with 100% financing that is 26 small businesses we have created with over $7million in capital" (2013 GhanaFest Brochure).

The *Chicago Dispatcher* of October 2013 had this caption: "The Department of Business Affairs and Consumer Protection (BACP) announce the sale of fifty (50) City of Chicago taxicab medallions by a bid auction. The 2013 Taxicab Medallion Auction begins September 16, 2013 and ends October 28, 2013. The upset price, the minimum bid allowable, is **$360,000.00** (U.S. Dollars) per taxicab medallion."

The taxi business is the most flexible job one can find in this part of the world. The flexibility allows one to have independence of mind and time to manage one's personal and family life. A chauffeur does not need permission to take a break, and his break isn't truncated by time. A chauffeur can take leave any time that's convenient to him and for as long as he wishes. It is a student-friendly job that gives students the ability to readily schedule their time to work as well as attend classes. One does not need to ask for permission from a manager or supervisor before taking a leave of absence from work. One will not have to call two hours in advance to inform his supervisor that he cannot work on a particular day or will be thirty minutes late. You don't need to punch time in or out. You are by yourself all the time. There is no age limit for retirement. Some people even retire from their jobs before entering the chauffeur profession.

Some drivers work only during the night so they can take care of their children during the day while their wives work.

Incentives: Driver Excellence Award

The City of Chicago has a program that awards conscientious drivers. Each year, the Taxi Driver Excellence Award is presented to the most dedicated driver selected from a lot of nominees. Nominees are chosen based on their service to the disabled community and commitment to drive a wheelchair-accessible vehicles. The winner receives an award and also a free taxicab medallion, which is currently sold for more than $350,000. The 2012 recipient of the award was Imran Mirza. Chicago Mayor Rahm Emanuel made the presentation on February 7 at driver recruitment day at Olive Harvey College. Mirza was chosen by a panel led by Commissioner Karen Tamley from the mayor's office.

"In dedicating his career to drive a wheelchair accessible taxicab, Mr. Mirza provides not just a service but his work gives members of the disabled community the freedom that they deserve to comfortably travel the streets of Chicago. I hope to see more drivers follow his example" said by Karen Tamley from Mayor's Office for people with disabilities at a press release on February 7, 2013. (*Chicago Dispatcher*, February 2013).

With the emergence of ride-sharing companies like uberX, Lyft, and Sidecar competing with Taxis for passengers, the price level of a Taxi Medallion is in the process of decline.

Challenges of Chicago Taxi Drivers

Notwithstanding the flexibility of the work, it can be very stressful at times. The multifarious stress comes from personnel at BACP who monitor the business to ensure that drivers are in compliance with its rules and regulations. They also ensure that drivers who are not licensed chauffeurs do not drive taxis, and even licensed chauffeurs must have in their possession their lease agreements during working hours. Moreover, they ensure that the equipment is in good condition and your taxi is clean, both inside and outside. A driver can be cited or ticketed for any of these violations. They are empowered to remove the medallion and meter of any taxi that fails to show up for its biannual inspection, thus depriving the driver the right to operate that vehicle as taxi. The medallion owner will have to pay some fine in addition to the suspension of the vehicle for some days or weeks.

During the inspection time, drivers go through very stressful and frustrating situations. Some frustrations emanate from being given a ticket or being asked to retest in some instances where the failure has absolutely nothing to do with equipment malfunction or safety. A retest alone costs the owner seventy-five dollars in addition to any fine the driver might be subjected to.

In one instance, a driver failed because he forgot to write the name of his affiliation on the information sheet. A small tear in the leather cover of the seats can cause a failure at inspection. In addition to these stressful situations, the medallion owner has to spend a lot of money, while the driver will have to suspend normal duties for some days in order to fulfill the inspection assignment. Any defective equipment must be replaced. Until the inspection is passed, drivers are haunted by the outcome of their toil. Officials from BACP frequent airports, hotels, train stations, and other taxi staging areas to check on drivers and their cars. Another group that puts stress on drivers is the Chicago Police Department, which ensures that drivers operate in compliance with the city and state rules of the road. The police can pull you over for reckless driving, failure to obey traffic rules, speeding, or any moving violations. You can be ticketed to pay the appropriate fine or penalty. The police also check on equipment malfunction as well as passenger and pedestrian safety.

Driving in a big city such as ours, one major problem is the pedestrians. Some will cross the street irrespective of the traffic signals. Others have their mobile phones pressed to their ears and look nowhere while crossing the street. A few will be reading and writing messages while crossing the street, paying no attention to the traffic signals. During the morning or evening rush hour when people are coming out from their trains or going to board the trains, they cross the streets in multitudes, thus holding traffic to their satisfaction. The bicyclists have their own set of rules of the road and crisscross traffic with total disregard for traffic signals. They ride in any direction that is convenient for them. Another group is the few uncompromising bus drivers who will not yield to cabbies. In all these situations, the taxi driver has to take every precaution to prevent an accident. Any accident is usually blamable on the driver, especially cabbies. The most awful situation is the other drivers, especially some taxi drivers, who are in the habit of crossing or overtaking other cabbies with the intention of picking up the next available fare, thereby sometimes causing unnecessary accidents.

The Chicago Department of Transportation estimates that more than three thousand people are hit by vehicles in Chicago each year. Generally, most passengers behave themselves, but sometimes taxi drivers have a bad passenger who may give the driver problems, especially on weekends when some become drunk. One Friday night I picked up a young man. He just told me the intersection to his destination but no specific address. When I got to the intersection and stopped, this young man was dead asleep, and any effort to wake him up proved futile. My only alternative was to call the police. It took the two police officers more than five minutes to wake him up. The police demanded his ID, but he could not produce one. This young man was in the country illegally because he had overstayed his visa. The police took him into custody. I felt bad about the situation, but I had no better option than to call in the police. Because of his expired visa, the likelihood of the young man being deported was high.

Some would be late for their appointments but would want the driver to make amends for their shortfalls, sometimes suggesting the driver violated traffic signal to their advantage. Some taxi drivers may at times cause their own problems while making a mad rush for a fare. In its quest to create an avenue of revenue, the city has set up a special court to prosecute offending drivers, especially cabbies. In one out of five cases, offenders will be found not guilty. Either way, you will have to pay a fine, and, in some cases, you are also required to attend remedial classes. Some legal practitioners are always ready to defend offenders but at a cost. Sometimes drivers need their services in order to protect their chauffeur licenses, because it is one's livelihood in this city.

Oftentimes, passengers start a conversation with funny questions. "You have an accent. Where are you from originally? Why did you come to the United States? Why did you settle in Chicago? Do you like it here? What is the weather like in your country?" The questions would continue: "Are you married? Do you have children? If so, how many? Is your family here? Do you visit home regularly? What is the government like in your country?"

If your passenger happened to come from Europe, then the conversation would shift to soccer, with some mentioning the most renowned Ghanaian international soccer players. Those who have traveled to other parts of the world generally behave nicely to foreigners, especially when they know that more than 90 percent of taxi drivers in Chicago are foreigners.

I once picked up four white passengers, and incidentally, the one who sat with me in the front seat greeted me in Twi, which is a local Ghanaian language. We continued our conversation in Twi. This man said he had lived in Ghana for eighteen years at Nsawam, Swedru, and Kintampo. Some people readily recognize my accent and tell me that I come from West Africa and ask which country.

On February 19, 2009, as I was driving southbound at exactly 1120 N. La Salle Street at about eleven thirty in the morning, a truck ran into my car. My car was sandwiched between the truck and the concrete curb. An ambulance transported me to Northwestern Memorial Hospital emergency department where I was admitted for observation and treatment for minor injuries.

According to city rules, for the safety of passengers, the rear seat must be fully occupied before a passenger can sit in the front seat. The risks involved in this business include robbery and sometimes murder, which is not limited to the United States alone. Though some chauffeurs have driven a taxi for more than three decades with virtually no bad incidents, not all are lucky. Some have been robbed, at times at gunpoint or knifepoint, and a few have been murdered in the course of their work.

The *Chicago Dispatcher* of January 2015 carried this headline: "Chicago Taxi Driver Murdered – Suspect in Custody." The story stated that Chicago taxi driver Chinedu Madu had been shot in the chest on the 1200 block of S. Albany Avenue at 8:45 p.m. on January 8, 2015. Chicago Police say the motive was robbery. Mr. Madu was taken to Mt. Sinai Hospital where he was pronounced dead.

Even in a relatively small and supposedly peaceful country like Ghana, one sometimes reads about a taxi driver being wounded or murdered. The website Ghanaweb.com of January 4, 2014, had this caption: "Police hunt for 3 women who stabbed a cabbie and stole his car. This incident occurred at Senfi near Bekwai in Ashanti Region of Ghana, where three ladies attacked a taxi driver and finally drove away with his taxi-cab."

Chapter 12

My Next Trip

My Second Visit to Ghana

I had planned to visit Ghana in August 2010, but an unfortunate incident occurred. My older brother Zakariya Adjei bin Sadik, also known in the family as Yaw Kordie and popularly called Master Zak in my village, died on Sunday, July 4, 2010. It was devastating news to me and the whole family. He had undergone a successful prostate surgery at a hospital in Atonsu-Kumasi. What made it more painful was that I'd had a conversation with him on that Sunday at about seven o'clock in the evening Ghana time. He told me that he would be discharged from the hospital the following Tuesday, and he would call me after he had been discharged. To my utter surprise, I received a call from one of his sons, Mahmud Adjei, the following Monday morning. He said my brother had died the previous night. According to sources at the hospital, he fell while using the restroom and bled profusely. There was no doctor on duty to attend to him instantly. By the time a doctor arrived, he had died. In fact, it was a very bitter pill to swallow.

For some time, I could not contain my sadness over the situation and wept all the time. As a Muslim, he was buried on the third day, and I knew definitely that there was no time for me to view his remains. The matter ended just like that. I know that if the same thing had happened elsewhere in any advanced country, the hospital would have been sued for negligence, and an appropriate compensation would have been paid to his survivors, but not in Ghana.

I then planned my visit home to coincide with the time the Ahmadiyya Mission would gather to read his testament, which normally takes place four months after the person's demise. In my brother's case, the time was scheduled for November 14, 2010. Incidentally, his eldest daughter, Elizabeth Mensah, was getting married in Leeds, England, on October 16, 2010. In view of my niece's marriage, I planned my trip to Ghana in such a way that I could also attend the marriage ceremony.

As a holder of American passport, I had to apply for a visa from the Ghana Embassy in Washington to enable me to enter Ghana. Conversely, I did not need a visa to enter England. I left Chicago on a British Airways flight from O'Hare International Airport at 5:40 p.m. Chicago time. Our flight landed at the London Heathrow International Airport the following morning. When I passed through the British Immigration Service at Heathrow International Airport, my passport was stamped with this inscription: "Leave to enter for six months. Employment and Recourse to Public Funds Prohibited."

After going through the immigration processes, I boarded a bus bound for Leeds. The fare from London to Leeds was eighty pounds. We passed through such historic towns as Coventry, Sheffield, and others and eventually reached Leeds. My brother-in-law Agyeman met me at the Leeds bus station and took me home. It was a very exciting moment when I saw my brother's daughter and his uncles Agyeman and Alex with their families. We had not seen each other for a very long time.

After the customary greetings, they led me to a place where I was to lodge. My hosts were Mr. and Mrs. Patrick Mensah, along with their two children Emily and Kwaku, who lived just a few blocks apart. In fact, I stayed with a warmhearted family. Mrs. Susanna Mensah, especially, provided me with such services that I felt really at home for the week I stayed with them. I wished I could stay for a much longer time. The traditional marriage rite was performed on Saturday, October 16, in the morning and was followed by the wedding later that afternoon. The church service was performed the next day. I used the remaining days to visit places of interest in downtown Leeds. I left Leeds on October 20 for London to continue my journey to Ghana on the same British Airways flight.

We arrived at the Kotoka International Airport at nine o'clock that night. Waiting for me at the airport was my lifelong friend Kwadwo Antwi (Bob), who took me home. I spent the night at Tema and left for Kumasi the following day. My good friends Abdullah Sam and Rockson Fosu were waiting patiently for me at a spot in Kumasi. Finally, I joined Mr. Sam at his residence where eventually I spent the rest of my holidays. Accompanied by my great friends, we traveled to my village, Anyanso, the next Saturday, October 23.

As soon as news of my arrival spread through the village, it was mourning revisited. People both young and old were crying and wailing; all poured into my late brother's residence. Family members and sympathizers gathered in the house for the traditional exchange of greetings. As a matter of fact, I could not contain my emotions but rather kept sobbing. My friends left for Kumasi in the evening. The next morning, I attended the morning prayers (*Fajr Salat*) and after the prayer, the traditional greetings started. In the midst of that, I broke down again on seeing a different person sitting on my late brother's place during prayers. It reminded me of his image. I could not utter a word. His wife joined me in the weeping at the mosque.

At My Ancestral Home

Accompanied by my oldest brother Hakeem Agyei Twum, my oldest sister Fatima, some friends and family members, I went to our ancestral home to greet my ailing uncle Kwaku Tawiah. Thereafter, we went to the palace to greet the chief and elders and to thank them for giving a fitting burial and funeral service to my late brother. Born and bred at Anyanso, my brother remained at Anyanso from 1973 when he was posted there as a class teacher till his death in 2010. He was a class teacher at Anyanso Local Authority Middle School and became the head teacher of that school. He later became the second head teacher of the Ahmadiyya Primary School, which was established in the mid-1980s. In fact, he was one of the people who helped in the establishment of the Ahmadiyya Primary School at Anyanso. Later when the school reached the junior secondary school level, he became the head of the school until his retirement in 2005.

On his assumption as a class teacher at the village, he was a member of the Town Development Committee and remained as such until the concept of the Community Assembly Member was introduced. At that time, he decided to run for the new position and won. He served for two terms. He was an agent for the National Electoral Commission at Anyanso, Anumso, and Freboye electoral area, registering voters, presiding during election years, and recording results after the elections. He was the imam of the Anyanso Ahmadiyya Community, eventually rising to become the head of the Amansie Circuit of the Mission. He was really a pillar of the community.

He was a peacemaker and an arbiter in interpersonal and communal issues. People would go to him for assistance and advice at any time of the day, and he was always prepared to assist. He was often with the chief and elders, offering advice and assistance. He was a staunch member of the Ahmadiyya Muslim Community in Ghana, such that there was no event of the mission that he would not attend, no matter where it was in the country. It was therefore not surprising that upon his death he was given a hero's burial and funeral at Anyanso. Multitudes of people from far and near, including the Ahmadiyya community, teachers, and people from all the surrounding villages, attended his funeral ceremony. A delegation from the Ashanti Regional Headquarters of the Ahmadiyya Mission, led by the regional chairman, Mr. Hakeem Baidoo, as well as Mr. I.B. Mohammed, attended the funeral celebration. Also in attendance was a delegation from the Amansie circuit of the mission led by the current circuit missionary and the former circuit missionary, Mr. Hakeem Agyei. His death was devastating to our family, the people of Anyanso, the surrounding communities, and the Ahmadiyya Muslim Community.

On some occasions during my visit, I took some time off to visit my alma mater, Ahmadiyya Secondary School to share memories of the past with my colleagues still on the staff, though the majority had retired or transferred by then. I was highly impressed with the infrastructural development and the maintenance of discipline, academic progress, and achievements in sports.

On October 26, I left Anyanso for Kumasi where I stayed with Mr. Sam. Two days later, I traveled to Accra to attend the marriage and wedding ceremony of my niece, Faustina Anokye. The marriage rite was performed in the morning at the residence of my elder cousin, Hon. Kwadwo Kyei Frimpong. The wedding took place at Tema Roman Catholic Church. I spent the days with my cousin Kwadwo Kyei Frimpong and his wife, Agnes Kyei Frimpong, in Accra and returned to Kumasi on October 30, 2010.

My ailing uncle Kwaku Tawiah died on November 1, so the next day I had to travel back to Anyanso to mourn with the family. I remained at Anyanso till the one-week celebration of his death before returning to Kumasi. On November 14, 2010, a delegation of the Ahmadiyya Community from both the regional office and Amansie circuit, headed by the circuit missionary, family members, the widows and their children, my friend Sam, and some community members, gathered at my late brother's residence to read his last testament. That event concluded my brother's activity in life.

Back to Chicago

On November 29, I left Kumasi for Accra in preparation for my return trip to Chicago. I traveled to Accra with my daughter Hanna Aboagye and her three children. She had been scheduled for a follow-up interview at the American Embassy on November 30, 2010. I left the shores of Ghana and headed back to America on December 2, 2010, which coincided with the thirty-sixth birthday of my daughter. Aboard the British Airways with a stopover at London's Heathrow International Airport, I arrived at Chicago's O'Hare International Airport at twelve thirty in the afternoon. My holiday ended with my arrival in Chicago. Waiting for me at the airport were my wife and some of my children. I reached home safely by the grace of God.

As compared to my previous trip to Ghana, the heat in the immigration center of Kotoka International Airport had been rectified. An air-conditioner had been installed to mitigate the heat that we had previously encountered. Communication system had also seen improvement due to the use of mobile phones. Road transportation had gotten better except for traffic jam, especially in the cities. The negative aspect of this trip was the upsurge in robberies. One afternoon while we were in town, Mr. Sam's wife called to say that our residence had been burgled and the thief had gotten away with some cash.

I had the opportunity to meet some family members and friends whom I had not seen for many years, either through wedding or the funeral celebrations.

I had the privilege of donating two sets of jerseys and footballs to the two junior secondary schools in my village. In addition, I donated a set of jerseys and a football to the only senior secondary school at Asiwa, our district capital. I also donated some crutches and a few medical items to the local clinic. My wife travels home more than me, and any time she traveled to Ghana, we shipped some used clothing ahead of her visit, which she distributed to the needy in the village. This philanthropic practice was initiated by Nana Akwaasi Addae, the ex-Asantefuohene of Chicago.

In June 2012 the present head of the worldwide Ahmadiyya Muslim Community in the person of Hazrat Mirza Masroor Ahmad - Khalifatul Masih V paid a visit to the *jama'at* (community) in the US Midwest. He visited the various mosques in the Midwest. He concluded his visit by addressing the sixty-fourth annual convention of the US *jama'at*. The sixty-fourth *jalsa salana* (annual convention) was held at the Pennsylvania Farm Show Complex and Expo Center in Harrisburg, Pennsylvania, from June 29 to July 1. I attended the yearly convention where I met with some old friends and acquaintances from Ghana.

CHAPTER 13

---•◦◆◦•---

THE GHANAIAN COMMUNITY IN CHICAGO

This book will not be complete if I fail to pay a glowing tribute to the earliest Ghanaian immigrants who settled and made this gorgeous city of Chicago their home. These pioneers, some of whom came on student or visitor visas, studied hard, and now some of them occupy positions of authority in various establishments. These first immigrants brought their spouses, children, relatives, and friends, and by and by, the Ghanaian population began to increase in Chicago. Currently, the Ghanaian population in Chicago is between twenty thousand and twenty-five thousand by a conservative estimate.

The greatest relief any sojourner can get is to have a secure, reliable, and comfortable place to lodge, and these earliest settlers in Chicago made this possible to the new Ghanaian immigrants. They were ready to offer assistance, in cash and kind, to any new Ghanaian immigrant. Those in positions of authority assisted the new arrivals with processing their documents, learning the geography of the city, looking for shelter, and acquiring jobs.

The Pioneers

These earliest residents experienced many problems during the initial stages of their stays. These problems included job acquisition, effective communication in a foreign land, procurement of food items and accommodations, and even interaction, among other things. In spite of the numerous problems these pioneers faced, they remained resolute and made life meaningful not only for themselves but for their spouses, children, friends, and extended family members. Some of them suffered deceit and disappointment from family members and friends with regard to investments they intended to undertake. The only form of communication available to them at that time with their loved ones back in Ghana was through letter writing, which took weeks or even months to reach recipients. In the case of an emergency, sending a telegram was the only option.

From the interviewers' account which included A.C. Eddie Quartey, Naa Issah Samori, Nana Jerry Addae Baffour, Mrs. Sally Owusu and others, the early Ghanaians who first settled in Chicago in the 1960s and 1970s were: Messrs A.C. Eddie Quartey, Rev. Albert W. Mensah, Emmanuel Boafo Papafio, Joseph Appiah, John Abbeyea, Alhaji Adjei Okoe, Joe Di Archisco Ocloo, Alhaji Wahabi Tijani, Richard Allotey, Obuabadan Sowah Botchway, Tita Pongo, Andrews Bortey, Frank Bonney, Jonas Reindorf, Ernest Oware, Atta Darku, Dr. Felix Legge, Thomas D. Laryea, El Adnan, Alhaji Sulemana Giwa, Dr. Andrews Davis, Dr. Evans Fiakpui, Dr. Emmanuel Bansah, Fred Buckle, Alhaji Gariba Issaka, Solomon Manson, Alex Annan, Naa Issah Samori, E. Akuetteh Williams, Kojo Renner, Atta Krufi, Stephen Somuah, Frank Adu, Francis Duah, Nana Akwasi Appiah, Nana Jerry Addai Baffour, Nana Osei Abebrese, Nana Kwaku Duah, Joseph Kudjo Adigbli, Mrs. Patience Amui Adigbli, Nana Bennett Barnie Agyeman, Mrs. Betty

Agyeman, Robert Yaw Barima Mintah, Mrs. Grace Mintah, Nana Kwame Boakye-Yiadom, Mrs. Janet Boakye Yiadom, Ms. Grace Amarteifio, Ms. Kukua Eshun, and Ms. Alice Ogbarmey-Tetteh.

Others included Joseph Menya, Alex Prempeh, Edmond Otoo, Nana Wiafe Ababio, J.C. Tetteh, Malas Osafo, Gilbert Ntow, Kojo Gbogbotsi, Kafui Amegashie, Gilbert Bortey, Akwasi Sarpong, Nii Mensah Legge, Godfred Annang, Michael Amegashie, Olu Johnson, Billy Balogun, Philip Owusu, Nii Ablorh Jackson, Ernest Welbeck, Muda Sanusi, Sarfo Kantanka, Victor Clottey, Tanko Brimah, Benjamin A. Ale, Ben Anaman, John Bruce Amartey, Ishmael Seye, John Allen, Willie Grant Acquah, Sam Owoo-Batlett, Ebenezer Lamptey, John Owusu, Philip B. Owusu, Thomas Ampofo, Nana Wiafe Akenten, Frank Quabena Antwi-Barfi, Nana Opoku Ansah, Dr. George Ofori-Attah, Mrs. Felicia Ofori-Atta, Kwadwo Antwi-Mensah, Alhaji Tahiru Mohammed, Anthony Djondo, Jonas Bonsu, Ago Flether, Mrs. Roberta Amarfio, Ms. Diana Ahia, Ms. Adjoa Pinaman, Ms. Susan Arthur, Ms. Evelyn Dowuona, Mrs. Anorkor Owusu, Elizabeth Ahia, Messrs Paul Owusu, Alfred Akwasi Agyeman, Aidoo Frank, Aidoo Victoria, Mrs. Nana Kobiwa, Kwame Boateng, Sampson Akotuah, Agnes Akotuah, Mrs. Nana Amma Akyaah, Augustine Kwabena Afriyie, Mrs. Comfort Afriyie, Dapaah Stephen, Kwasi Bekoe, Mrs. Elizabeth Abena Bekoe, Anthony Kwarteng, Mrs. Mary Kwarteng, Gifty Lawson Alhaji Ibrahim Samuel Addai, and Martha Addai.

Though some of the pioneer immigrants have relocated to other states, different countries, or back to Ghana and others have passed away, their contributions to the growth of the Ghanaian community in Chicago must be recognized and appreciated. They paved the way for successive Ghanaian immigrants to have a very fruitful settlement in Chicago. These early settlers were mostly living in the south side of Chicago, predominantly in the Hyde

Park neighborhood, but some later moved to live in the northern neighborhoods and the suburbs. Two categories of Ghanaians in the diaspora can be identified: those who decide to make America their home permanently and others who decide to return to Ghana after retirement. Some of those in the first category pay periodic visits to the motherland. The people in the latter group make some investments at home toward their retirement.

The plight of immigrants has now changed as a result of science and technology, which have made the world a global village. Communication to any part of the world takes just a few seconds through mobile phone calls, text messages, e-mail, and other devices, as opposed to the situation of the pioneer immigrants. Their meals were only American or the foreign food items. Currently Ghanaian foodstuffs are easily available through the efforts of some Ghanaian entrepreneurs. Such grocery stores as Makola Supermarket by Nana Yaw Adu Gyamfi, Kaneshie Supermarket by Ms. Esther Koranteng, and the Blessed Homeland Supermarket by Ms. Joyce Karikari are just a few of what's available in Chicago. These stores have helped Ghanaians to get authentic Ghanaian foodstuffs to their homes. Also, the United African Market by George Amoh in Bolingbrook, a southwest suburb of Chicago, offers similar services to Ghanaian residents in Bolingbrook and nearby suburbs. Grace African and Palace Gate are restaurants that also offer Ghanaians very appetizing and genuine traditional meals, as well as P.K's Catering and Restaurant in suburban University Park, which is owned by Kwadwo Baffour, also known as Chef Kujo.

The Professionals

Ghanaian professionals are spread out in Chicago and its suburbs. They include lawyers (many are immigration attorneys), accountants, architects, teachers in pretertiary institutions, university teachers, doctors, dentists, journalists, engineers, IT specialists, nurses, chauffeurs, priests, pastors, dressmakers, barbers, hair braiders, and business professionals. Ghanaian students abound in institutions at all levels of the education system in Chicago and the suburbs.

Some of these professionals have their own establishments. Following is a list of some I am familiar with: The *African Spectrum Newspaper* is published by Berko Akoto Owusu and informs Ghanaians, as well as non-Ghanaians, about news from Africa and diaspora. Sankofa Online is a website created and administered by Reuben Hadzide, a former president of the Ghana National Council. This website furnishes the Ghanaian community in Chicago and elsewhere with general news, Chicago news, entertainment, event updates, photo galleries of events, and much more. He attends almost every Ghanaian function, taking photographs of celebrants and attendees alike. Ghanaians are also fortunate to have the Legend Media Network (LMN) established by an enterprising young journalist named Isaac K. Boateng (popularly called En'Kay Boateng).

According to En'Kay Boateng,

> The LMN has been very active within the Chicago African and Ghanaian Communities as well as Ghanaian communities across the United States. The team has also worked assiduously to build strong links with our homeland, Ghana. This link is exhibited by an exchange of programs with some Frequency Modulation (FM) Radio and Television Stations in Ghana. LMN is primarily a non-profit community-oriented media organization whose purpose is to provide a voice for the voiceless and affiliated with the

African Diaspora, who has previously been without adequate access to broadcast media and representation. We strive to continue this through presenting and exposing the Diaspora in a positive and realistically concise approach; along with the pursuit of involvement through the broad-based African community elements to guarantee that access. We have created movements such as Ghana Africa Explosion (GAE), and Voices of Ghanaians Abroad (VOGA) that will produce community events periodically that will advocate, educate, entertain and provide a voice for our communities in the Diaspora.

These events bring some awareness and raise funds in support of a research that is to help fight against injustice and socio-economic problems in developing countries, especially, Ghana, as well as adding on to the developments in our community on a foreign land. The community events hosted by LMN will bring our people together to lighten the burdens of our struggle in a foreign land and do our part to reflect our nation and people in a positive light on the global stage. Its programs include community announcements, live discussions on topical issues in Ghana and among Ghanaians in the Diaspora, issues like marriage, immigration, religion and many more.

The board of directors at LMN are Isaac Boateng, Dr. Paul Yeboah Jr., Akosua Morgan, Joyce Asamoah-Boateng, and Paul Reed. Presenters include En'kay Boateng, Kwabena Owusu (Hot

FM-Ghana), Cephas Mensah (HOT FM-Ghana), Paul Kwame Ntim (HOT FM-Ghana), Oheneba John Nti, Abena Darko (Ghana), and Kelvin Asamoah-Baah. Guest presenters include Attah Adu-Gyamfi (Aban), Steve Dei, Berko Akoto Owusu, Bruce Nimo, Samuel Okyere, Francis Asante, Mrs. Jennifer Nartey, Oheneba Nti, Kelvin A. Baah, Nana Yaw Marfo, Yaa Ledzi, Comfort (Efe), D.J. Odikro, and Obaa Yaa.

The Establishments

Other establishments include Akainya's Gallery by Prof. Samuel Akainya; Oakley Construction Company Inc., Chicago's premier Ghanaian owned and operated general construction company since 1984 with Messrs Augustine Afriyie as president and late Anthony Kwateng as vice-president; the All Star of Chicago, a mechanic workshop owned by Emmanuel Owusu; and Annaka Enterprises, a wholesale and distributor of Vlisco (real Dutch hollandaise) and African-style fabrics with two locations in Chicago.

In the same vein, we have Abena's clothing center, "where fashion comes to life," owned and operated by Abena Addae. She designs and makes fabrics for men and women. She also retails Holland prints, laces, and Galle and African fabrics like Kente. Julsam Fashions in suburban Bolingbrook is managed by Mrs. Juliana Sam, who also designs pieces of clothings.

Some individuals and groups also provide door-to-door shipping services of autos, as well as personal and commercial items, to Ghana and other parts of the world. They include African Global Logistics Company, owned by Charles Slim; K.E. Shipping, owned by Abuba; Conship, owned by Yolanda Dunn; and Global Stewards Company Limited, owned by Ben Ayensu and Kofi Kwakye. Masters Travel managed by Steve Osei Assibey also provides travel needs of Ghanaians in Chicago and elsewhere. Upon request, he searches for flight schedules and buys tickets for prospective travelers to any part of the world. He also has a shipping business that handles autos and personal belongings for clients.

For medical establishments, we have the dental office of Dr. Aaron Ohemeng in suburban Oak Park; Universal Health Clinics in Chicago, managed by Dr. Michael O. Appiagyei and providing medical services in internal medicine and pediatrics; Korle Bu Medical Center in Chicago with Dr. John A. Awah serving as president and CEO; and OSAFO Health Care Clinic Inc. in Bolingbrook, with Dr. Seth Osafo as the proprietor and CEO. Furthermore, there is Medex Healthcare Inc., whose president and CEO is the young entrepreneur Nelson Hodogbey. This clinic provides health services to Ghanaians and non-Ghanaians alike. The Gold Coast Home Health Inc. performs similar services; Reuben Hadzide, former president of the Ghana National Council, is a partial proprietor and administrator.

Religious Organizations

In order to satisfy the spiritual needs of the Ghanaian community, a number of churches and religious organizations abound in Chicago. The congregations of the various churches worship at different locations and times. The Ghanaian Catholic Community has Dr. George Osei Assibey-Mensah as the president; African Community United Methodist Church is led by Rev. Frederick Lartey; Ebenezer United Church is led by Rev. Dr. Kofi Noonoo; Redemption Presbyterian Church of Ghana is led by Rev. Samuel Afoakwa-Badu; Grace Episcopal Church is led by Fr. Canon Albert Mensah; Ghanaian Presbyterian Church of Chicago is led by Rev. James Acquaah; Apostolic Church International-USA,

Church of Pentecost is led by Rev. Michael Agyeman-Amoako; and Winners House of Praise is led by Pastor Nat Awuni; Living Comfort Ministries is led by Pastor Dzifanu Agbenya.

Others include the Christ Oasis Ministries with Dr. Isaac Paintsil as the senior pastor; Christ Pentecostal International Church is led by Rev. Seth Dolley; Bread Of Life Ministries is led by Dr. Mary Adufah; AME Zion Church is led by Rev. Grace H. Frempong; St. Andrew Episcopal Church is led by Father Canon Robert Koomson; ACME Ministries is led by Pastor Samuel Aidoo; Evangelical Presbyterian Church is led by Catechist Paul Adessu; Church of the Living God is led by Pastor Victor Owusu-Teng; and World Life Kingdom Ministries is led by Pastor Anthony Mensah. The Church of Ghanaian Community has the following leaders: Rev. Akwasi Yeboah Amponsah, Rev. Nana Owusu Bempah, Rev. Emmanuel Amonoo, and Evangelist Joseph Kwamina Sam. The Seventh Day Adventist Church also has its presence in Chicago. The various churches have come together to constitute the Council of Ghanaian Churches (CGC) with Rev. Dr. Kofi Noonoo as the president and Dr. Gabriel Amoateng Boahen as the vice president.

The Ghanaian Muslim Community also worships at various mosques (*masjids*) across Chicago. They include Masjid Fathir on 4700 S. Woodlawn, Masjid Tabak on 1300 N. Clybourn Avenue, and Masjids Haske on 4819 S. Ashland. The Ahmadiyya Muslim Mission has two Mosques located at 4500 S. Wabash on the east side and 2240 W. Van Buren on the west side of the city.

Social Activities

Ghanaians are not left out in the vibrant Chicago summer activities. The various associations and churches organize outdoor fraternity activities such as barbecues and music festivals. Individuals also observe birthday celebrations, baby showers, and engagement and wedding activities, at which the traditional Ghanaian hospitality is displayed to the utmost. In the event of death, Ghanaians express their condolences to the bereaved family by attending the funeral celebration. When death occurs in Chicago or any of the suburbs, people sympathize by going to the funeral home to view the body, attend the church service, and follow it up to the traditional funeral rite where they give out donations to support the bereaved family. A church service is organized to finalize the celebration. Most of the social and funeral celebrations are organized on Saturday nights to attract maximum attendance.

The importance of the master of ceremonies at such celebrations cannot be overemphasized. Celebrated MCs include Kwaku Boateng (Barfour Sakyi), Emmanuel Boafo Papafio, Sammy Young, Kwasi Amponsah Yeboah, Mrs. Jennifer Osei Nartey, Abdul Brimah, and Nana Yaw Marfo. Others are N.K Boateng, Steve Dei, Nana Kwame Frimpong, Kwaku Antwi, Mrs. Elizabeth Mills, Michael Opoku (Cosby Michael), Bismark Briamah, Ms. Akua Agyeman, and many more. These MCs make the events more lively and entertaining. The works of the MCs are complemented by the disc jockeys like DJ Bonsu, DJ Odikro, DJ Benghazi, DJ Master "Pee," and DJ Chief. Videographers include Messrs Samuel Owusu of NANEFFE Video Productions and Kudjo Akoto Asomani. The photographers include Reuben Hadzide of Sankofa fame (sometimes his sons substitute for him), Psalms Media Network by Sam Okyere, Peter Wilson, and a lot more. The Nyansapo band led by Smart Frempong also provides live band entertainment by seasoned Ghanaian musicians of the past like Dan Boadi, Joe Owusu, and others. Gospel artists such as Nat Awuni, Minister Appau Kenneth (Biggy), and Victoria Adjei (Mama Vicky) occasionally entertain Ghanaians with their brilliant and inspirational performances.

Ghana National Council

History

According to narrators like A.C. Eddie Quartey, Naa Issah Samori and others, the Ghana National Council started as a student organization in the early 1980s by the new and young Ghanaian immigrants who had arrived in Chicago during that period. Some of them came on student visas, while others arrived on visitor visas. The need for the young Ghanaians to come together to fraternize and share ideas and information culminated in the formation of the Ghana Students' Union (GSU). These young men were mostly located in the south side of Chicago, predominantly in the Hyde Park neighborhood. As the Ghanaian population in Chicago increased, the GSU expanded and evolved into the Ghana National Council (GNC) by the efforts of some personalities.

"According to A.C. Quartey, the mission of the Council was to serve the increasing Ghanaian Community and also to educate the Ghanaian-American youth as well as the Chicago public about the Ghanaian people – their culture and tradition. It also served as a medium to assist new immigrants and give support to those in need especially in times of sickness and bereavement."

A.C. Eddie-Quartey said that the formative periods of the GNC faced many challenges "then followed a long period of hiatus, when the community had no representation. During this time, two distinct organizations emerged that would become the nucleus of the GNC, the Ghana Chicago Club (GCC), (GaDangme based) and the Milenovisi Habobo (Ewe based)."

Thereafter, other ethnic organizations joined the membership of the GNC to make it a more vibrant organization. Dynamic personalities included Benjamin Annaman; Joseph Adigbli and his wife, Patience Adigbli; Alhaji Wahabi Tijani; Rev. Albert

Mensah; A.C. Eddie-Quartey; Benjamin Ale (deceased); Joseph Appiah; Rev. Kweku Lartey (deceased); Alhaji Baba Cisse; Godfred Annang; Kingsley Mensah; Ishmael Seye (deceased); Nana Wiafe Ababio; Obuabadan Sowah Botchway; Rev. A.A. Akrong; and Dan McKwartin (deceased). All aforementioned personalities played very prominent roles in nurturing the GNC to become what it is today, and their individual and collective contributions must be recognized and appreciated. (Source: Ghana.com/A.C.Eddie-Quartey)

My Membership of the Council

In November 2007, while driving for Gold Coast Taxi Association, Mr. John Henry Assabill asked me to join his executive body at the GNC of Metropolitan Chicago. Having known him for a relatively short time, I told him to give me some time to ponder over it. I accepted the request knowing very well that it was community work. The GNC of Metropolitan Chicago is the umbrella organization of all the Ghanaian organizations in Chicago. The council is composed of three representatives from each of the affiliate organizations of the Ghanaian community in Chicago. The affiliates include Asanteman Association, Brong Ahafo Association, Ewe Association, Fanti Benevolent Society, GaDangme Community Organization, Ghana Chicago Club, Ghana Northern Union, Haske Society, Kwahu United Association, Okuapeman Fekuw, Okyeman Association, Nzema Association, and Mmrantie Kuo. It was initially founded as a student organization in 1988 or thereabout but has developed over the years to become a vibrant Ghanaian Diaspora Organization, not only in America but the world over.

John Henry Assabill had just been elected as the new president of the GNC. The former president, Mr. Reuben Hadzide, had ended his term. Throughout his six-year term as president, officially from January 2008 to December 2013, I remained a member of the executive committee, having served as assistant secretary, secretary, and assistant financial secretary. My first attendance at the meeting of the council was on December 2, 2007, at Sixty-First Street and Michigan Avenue, which was the venue for the council meetings.

At one such meeting, vandals broke the windshields of four taxicabs owned by members that were parked outside the meeting place. It is an undeniable fact that Mr. John Henry Assabill had moved the venue of our meetings from a dungeon-like church basement to Ramada Hotel, a more serene and secure environment befitting the status of the council. Furthermore, he introduced the admission fees to GhanaFest celebrations to earn some revenue for the council.

GhanaFest is an annual festival of Ghanaians in Chicago that showcases the authentic Ghanaian culture and tradition. It is always held on the last Saturday of July. Mr. John Henry Assabill served the Ghanaian community as the president of the Ghanaian Taxi Drivers Association from 2000 to 2008, president of the GNC from 2008 to 2013, and the manager of the Gold Coast Taxi Association from 2003 to present. All these selfless accomplishments, he performed with dexterity.

During the 2013 GhanaFest celebration, which marked the silver jubilee celebration of the festival and the end of his tenure as president of the council, Mr. Assabill invited Daasebre Nana Osei Bonsu II, the *Omanhene* (paramount chief) of Asante Mampong Traditional area and the occupant of the Silver Stool of the kingdom of Asante, to address the gathering. According to the *African Spectrum Newspaper* of August 2013, volume 15, issue 5, "on this day, however, before the traditional chiefs and the queens arrive, spectators and well-wishers are treated to some of the amazing indigenous Ghanaian music available. The traditional leaders dress in gorgeous traditional clothes and sit in state to receive homage from various people. Vendors of all types are usually present at the park." (The *African Spectrum Newspaper* is published by a Ghanaian journalist named Berko Akoto Owusu of Bolingbrook.)

Leadership of the Council

Following is a list of the Leadership of the GNC of Metropolitan Chicago in chronological order:

- Joseph Kudjo Adigbli, president, 1984
- Rev. Dr. Kweku Lartey, secretary general, 1990 to 1993
- Alhaji Baba Cisse, president, 1993 to1996
- Pastor Nana Owusu Bempah, president, 1997 to 1998
- Clement Timpo, president, 1998 to 2004
- Dr. Yahya Abdallah, president, 2004
- Mrs. Elizabeth Abena Bekoe, president, 2004 to 2005
- Reuben Hadzide, president, 2005 to 2008
- John Henry Assabill, president, 2008 to 2014
- Ebenezer Antwi Nsiah, president, 2014 to the present

(Courtesy of A.C. Eddie-Quartey, Chairman, Ghana Chicago Club)

At the end of his first term of office in 2010, Pres. John Henry Assabill had the following as his executive members: Dr. George Ossei Assibey-Mensah (vice president), Sadik Bosompem Aboagye (secretary), John Henry Baffoe (treasurer), Ben Kodom Ayensu (financial secretary), Eugene Kwame Frimpong (publicity officer), Steve Dei (organizing secretary), Emmanuel Paa Kwasi Sam (business manager), Emmanuel Ankumah-Saikoom (welfare officer), George Asare Boafo (sergeant at arms), Ali Brimah (youth secretary), Veronica Farkye (assistant secretary), Godwin Asanga (assistant organizing secretary), Daniel Lamptey (assistant business manager), and Nana Yaw Marfo (assistant youth secretary). (source: 2010 GhanaFest brochure)

The following members served as the executive body at the end of John Henry Assabill's second and final term of office in 2013:

Dr. Mark Kutame (vice president), Belinda Adikie McKwartin (secretary), Joseph Henry Baffoe (treasurer), Ben Kodom Ayensu (financial secretary), Emmanuel Boafo Papafio (public relations officer), Frederica Buckman (organizing secretary), Hajia Mariam Issaka (business manager), Nelson Hodogbey (youth secretary), Philip Acquah (assistant secretary), John K. Otoo (assistant business manager), Sadik Bosompem Aboagye (assistant financial secretary), Jonathan Codjoe (welfare officer), Roney Kumi (assistant organizing secretary), Jennifer Osei-Nartey (assistant public relations officer), and George Asare Boafo (sergeant at arms). (source: 2013 GhanaFest brochure)

The current administration of President. Ebenezer Antwi-Nsiah has the following members forming the executive committee: Emmanuel Paa Kwasi Sam (vice president), Evelyn Antwi-Mensah (treasurer), Sadik Bosompem Aboagye (executive secretary), Fred Eddie-Quartey (business manager), Akua Kwateng-Bonsu (publicity secretary), Fred Dunnuu (financial secretary), Godwin Asanga (welfare secretary), Steve Dei (organizing secretary), Valentina Kwateng (assistant organizing secretary), and Eugene Kwame Frimpong (sergeant at arms). (source: 2014 GhanaFest brochure)

Composition of the Council

Notwithstanding the exit of the Ghana Nurses Association from the council, the council's membership has risen from eleven to thirteen as the Nzema Association of North America (Chicago chapter) and Mmrantie Kuo (a youth association) have recently joined the council. Each member association presents three representatives that make up the council. Most of the associations have their traditional leaders that reflect on the base of the association or organization.

The affiliations include:

- Asanteman Association has Nana Addae Baffour as Asantefuohene (chief), Ohemaa Abena Amponsah as Asantefuohemaa (queen), and Nana Yaw Asamoah as Kontihene (deputy chief).
- Brong-Ahafo Association has Nana Yaw Adu-Gyamfi as chief, Nana Abena Pokuah as queen, and Ben Kodom-Ayensu as president.
- Ewe Association has Togbe Simon Addo as chief, Mama Kyerebea Ameyibor as queen, and Steve Dei as president.
- Fanti Benevolent Society has Nana Kobina Korantsen as chief, Nana Efua Dansoah as queen, and Joseph Henry Baffoe as president.
- Ga-Dangme Community Organization has Nii Armah Akonfra I as chief, Naa Dedei Amobiye as queen, and Frederica Buckman as president.
- Ghana Chicago Club has A.C. Eddie Quartey as chairman, Fred Eddie Quartey as secretary and Dan Asem as representative.
- Ghana Northern Union has Naa Issah Samori as chief, Pagnaa Hajia Habiba Fuseini as queen, and Kassim Abubakari as president.
- Haske Society has Alhaji Suleman Giwa as chief, Magajia Sekina Mohammed as queen, and Alhaji Tijani Wahabi as president.

- Kwahu United Association has Nana Kwame Asamoah I as chief, Ohemaa Akosua Asantewaa as queen, and John Kesse as president.
- Okuapeman Fekuh has Nana Yirenkyi Bonsu as chief, Ohemaa Akosua Pokuah as queen, and Emmanuel Paa Kwasi Sam as president.
- Okyeman Association has Nana Akwafo Adu Brempong II as chief, Ohemaa Adwoa Tiwaa as queen, and Ms. Florence Mahama as president.
- Mmrantie Kuo has Edward Owusu as president and Francis Quartey and Fred Agyeman as representatives.
- Nzima Association has Dr. Samuel Akainya, Kofi Anaman, and Ennor Agyeman as representatives.

(source: 2014 GhanaFest brochure)

GhanaFest

GhanaFest is an annual festival of Ghanaians in Metropolitan Chicago that exhibits authentic Ghanaian traditions and culture. The cultural aspect is demonstrated by the traditional appearance of the chiefs and queens in their traditional outfits. They sit in state to receive homage or greetings from their "subjects" and the general public. Apart from the traditional dresses, a number of Ghanaian cuisines are displayed that enable the participants have the feeling of nostalgia. It is a period of merrymaking. Traditional drumming, music, and dancing are performed to entertain the participants, Ghanaians and non-Ghanaians alike. It is a complete replica of the Ghanaian tradition back home.

The history of GhanaFest as recorded by A.C. Eddie-Quartey is that: "In the summer of 1987, the Ghana-Chicago Club, a socio- economic group in collaboration with some leaders of

GaDangme in Chicago organized a celebration in August called 'Homowo' a festival of thanksgiving by the Ga tribe of Ghana. The celebration attracted most GaDangmes as well as a cross-section of Ghanaians and non-Ghanaians at the Jackson Park in Chicago's South Side." (source: 2014 GhanaFest brochure)

GhanaFest has been celebrated every year since 1988 on the last Saturday of July. The event begins at eleven o'clock in the morning and ends at ten o'clock at night. The event begins with the procession of the traditional leaders of the various associations. Prayers are offered by the Christian and Muslim leaders. Libation is poured by one of the linguists of the associations. These practices are in conformity with what pertains in Ghana on any important occasion.

The National Anthems of Ghana and the United States are sung. This is followed by the sprinkle of traditional *Kpokpoi* by the Ga Mantse. The president of the GNC president is introduced usually by the vice-president to the gathering who then delivers a welcome address. Normally, the vice president introduces the invited dignitaries. Led by the president, the dignitaries greet the traditional leaders who are seated in their tents, dressed in their gorgeous traditional clothes. These activities are usually interspersed with music by disc jockeys with traditional gospel music and cultural dancing. The traditional leaders, in turn, go and welcome the dignitaries. The guest of honor would thereafter deliver his speech.

Dignitaries at GhanaFest

Important personalities who have given speeches or attended GhanaFest celebrations include Flt. Lt. Jerry John Rawlings, former president of Ghana (2006); Pat Quinn, governor of Illinois (2010, 2013); Hon. S. K. Boafo, then Minister of Chieftaincy

Affairs in Ghana (2006, 2008); Hon. Daniel Ohene Agyekum, former Ghana Ambassador to United States (2010); Mayor Richard Daley; Hon. Albert Abongo, then Ghana's Minister for Water Resources (2009); Hon. Ignatius Baffour Awuah, Brong-Ahafo regional minister (2007); Dr. Paa Kwasi Ndoum, member of parliament for Elmina and Minister for Public Sector Reform (2007); Dr. Martin La Kumi, a dentist in Toronto, Canada, and then Ghana's Honorary Consular-General of Toronto-Canada (2006); and Dr. John A. Awah, proprietor of Korle Bu Medical Center.

Others have included Mr. Francis Adjirakor, trade attaché for the Ghana Embassy in the United States (2011); Daasebre Osei Bonsu II, Omanhene of Asante-Mampong Traditional Area in Ghana (2013); Messrs Michael Munami, Chicago Olympic Committee Coordinator (2009) Illinois Sen. Kwame Raoul; Alderman Will Burns, Fourth Ward; Alderman Willie B. Cochran, Twentieth Ward (2009); Messrs Chuck Bowen, formerly a special representative for African affairs to Mayor Richard Daley; and Arnold Romeo, director of African affairs, Illinois Department of Human Services, who frequently attended the GhanaFest celebrations. The CEO of Ghana Web Mr. Francis Akoto from Europe and Mr. Charles Nimo Ntiamoah-Mensah, popularly known as Mr. CNN, from New York City have also attended the GhanaFest celebrations. (Courtesy: John Henry Assabill, former President, Ghana National Council)

The following personalities have served as moderators for the GNC: Prof. George Osei Assibey-Mensah (Asanteman Association of Chicago and Midwest, 2008); Rev. Kwasi Amponsah-Yeboah (Brong-Ahafo Association, 2009); Dr. Mark Kutame (Ewe Association, 2010); Mr. John Otoo (Fanti Benevolent Society, 2011); Jonathan A. Codjoe (GaDagme Community Organization, 2012); Mr. Godwin Asanga (Ghana Northern Union, 2013);

Alhaji Bashiru Habib (Haske Society, 2014); and Mr. Stephen Somuah (Kwahu United Association, 2015).

The sponsors of GhanaFest are recognized at the event. In past years, some of these sponsors have included the Mayor's Office of Special Events, Western Union, MoneyGram, Eco Bank, Ghana Limited, *African Spectrum Newspaper*, Annaka Enterprises, Transit Funding LLC, Ghana Web, and Princeton Insurance. The event is usually under the stewardship of the public relations officer, the organizing secretary, and the master of Ceremonies, who give directions and announcements as the event progresses.

To kill boredom, GhanaFest is laced with performances by the various cultural dancing groups in and around Chicago. They include: Asanteman Association Adowa group, Ewe Association Borborbo group, Cincinnati GaDangme Kpanlogo group, Ohio Sankofa group, Fanti Benevolent Society's Fancy group, and Ghana Northern Union Cultural group, as well as some gospel singers. Ghanaian artists like Nana Boro and Shatta Wale have also been featured in some GhanaFest celebrations, but at a cost.

The climax of the occasion is the traditional dancing by the various associations. Led by the chiefs and queens, members of the various associations dance to their favorite music provided by the DJs while extending pleasantries to the other traditional leaders and the dignitaries. The format of the dancing procession is usually done by balloting at a general meeting of the assembly prior to the date of the event.

The associations are Asanteman Association, Brong-Ahafo Association, Ewe Association, Fanti Benevolent Society, Ga-Adangme Community Organization, Ghana Chicago Club, Ghana Northern Union, Haske Society, Kwahu United Association, Mmrantie Kuo, Nzema Association, and Okyeman. The African American group led by their chief usually participates in the GhanaFest celebrations. This group is made up of black

Americans who have considered Ghana their home. Some of them have been installed as chiefs in some Ghanaian communities. After the dancing procession, the DJ provides general music to entertain the crowd, usually the youth who display their exuberance.

GhanaFest attracts about five thousand participants, both Ghanaians and non-Ghanaians, from Chicago, the suburbs, other states, and abroad. Available records from ticket sales indicate that in 2010, GhanaFest attracted four thousand paid attendees, excluding complimentary tickets. Children younger than twelve are exempt from payment. It has been described as the largest Ghanaian cultural exposition in the world outside Ghana.

On the event ground, a large area is reserved for food vendors who prepare different Ghanaian and African cuisine to sell to the numerous attendees. Another area is occupied by other vendors that sell wares, including clothing, traditional dresses, African artifacts, and cassettes. The various associations sit in their tents opposite the high table of officials and the invited dignitaries and the performance stage of the DJ. Portable toilet facilities are provided for the gathering. The event that started as a free event with a grant from the city has now become a paid event, as the city has withdrawn its grant. It even charges for the facilities it provides for the organizers due to economic recession. As a result of the payment of a nominal entrance fee, the organizers have to fence the venue for the event.

In his welcome remarks at the twenty-fifth GhanaFest celebration on Saturday, July 27, 2013, the former president of the GNC, John Henry Assabill, said in part, "GhanaFest was born from a need to bring all Ghanaians together in a social setting to express ourselves and portray our rich traditional culture. Representative of such rich culture are our traditional chiefs assembled here today representing all the ten regions of Ghana. Each region is on display here to showcase the rich diverse culture of Ghana. This is a proud moment for all of us" (source: 2013 GhanaFest brochure).

The current president of the GNC, Ebenezer Antwi-Nsiah, in his maiden welcome message on the occasion of the twenty-sixth GhanaFest anniversary held on July 26, 2014, stated, "While we celebrate this anniversary let us be ambassadors of our beloved country wherever we go and make a difference in our attitude, our work and the way we help each other and our neighbors, which is the hallmark of our beloved country, Ghana" (Source: 2014 GhanaFest brochure).

CHAPTER 14

CONCLUSION

My Experiences

Ghana

In a very humble rural setting, I attended Anyanso Methodist Primary School and then transferred to Asiwa Presbyterian Middle School, because my village had no middle school by then. On completion of my elementary school in 1964, I had the opportunity to attend T. I. Ahmadiyya Secondary School, popularly called T.I. AMASS, Kumasi, between 1964 and 1970. I lived with people who were not my biological parents in Kumasi until I had the chance to go to the boarding house.

Having attained my secondary school education certificate in 1970, I had a brief uncertificated teaching appointment at a rural school, Nsuta Local Authority Primary School, in the Amansie District of the Ashanti Region. I then proceeded to complete my professional teaching course at Bagabaga Teacher Training College at Tamale in the northern region of Ghana. With the accomplishment of my postsecondary teaching course, I had a teaching appointment in my own village, Anyanso, where I worked for four years, from 1973 to 1977.

With an aspiration for higher education, I transferred from my village to Asokore Ahmadiyya Elementary School to the chagrin of my head teacher, my fellow teachers, and my community. I taught for two years at Asokore Elementary School, from 1977 to 1979. I then had the opportunity to attend University of Ghana–Legon for a diploma course in the Study of Religions and Philosophy in 1979. Upon completion of my course, I did a one-year national service assignment at T.I. AMASS from 1981 to 1982.

I then decided to travel to Nigeria for about three years. Upon my return to Ghana, I went back to T.I. AMASS to teach. I not only was a classroom teacher but had other duties as well. I stayed at T.I. AMASS for about fourteen years and then went back to the College of Education at Winneba for a degree in Social Studies Education. It was at Winneba that I won the American Diversity Visa Lottery that eventually enabled me and my family to migrate to America, where we began residing in Chicago, Illinois.

In Chicago I began working at a parking garage where I stayed for about four months before leaving to work at O'Hare International Airport for about seven years. At the same time, I had a part-time substitute teaching job, especially on my off days. Subsequently, I registered to take the professional chauffeur course and finally became a professional chauffeur, which I have done until now.

The advancement of science and technology has made the world a global village, and my village is not an exception. It's a village that five decades ago could count on only one wooden vehicle that left for Kumasi at dawn and returned at dusk or sometimes late in the night. It is now a transportation hub for the surrounding communities. Cars and buses are readily available to transport people any time of the day. When I was in fourth grade, we were in the same classroom with students in fifth and sixth grades. Currently, my village boasts two public primary schools, as well as two public junior secondary schools. In addition, there are three private primary schools in the village. One of these private schools is Bio Memorial Children's Village, established by Nana Akwasi Addae, ex-Asantefuohene of Chicago.

All of this may be attributed to the population increase in the village. The resultant effect of the population increase is the expansion of the village for houses, schools, health facilities, and church buildings. The growth has been to the detriment of land for farming. The adverse consequence is that farmlands have now become limited due to the growing population, thus causing famine. This situation can be alleviated when the young people attend postelementary institutions, such as technical, vocational, and secondary schools elsewhere to enable them to acquire jobs after completion of their courses. The application of improved and high-yield seedlings to increase productivity may help with the situation.

The people in my village now drink water from pipes drilled from underground, which has replaced water from the streams that used to be the only source. There is now a clinic to meet the people's health-care needs. A modern market has been established by the Bosome-Freho District Assembly under the administration of Nana Kwame Adarkwah for the commercial needs of the people. Currently, people do not have to travel to Kumasi for such basic needs as grocery items, hardware, cement, and other related items.

The people now have access to electricity for lighting and other electronic devices, which had been denied us during my infancy and later years. The lack of the aforementioned amenities was an impediment to societal development. Some teachers refused postings to my village due to the absence of such amenities, especially the city dwellers.

On my recent visit to my ancestral village, I was amazed to find out the number of people who were using mobile phones. The telephone was an unheard of device during the time when I was at Anyanso, even as a teacher. Presently, some people would ask for mobile phones even more than money for their upkeep. It is now very easy to communicate, either way, with people in my village in the twinkle of an eye, any time of the day. The amazing result of technological advancement has enabled people to communicate from one part of the world to another, even in the remotest parts of the world. It is therefore not surprising that some people would call from my village and other parts of Ghana while we would be asleep. This situation is not peculiar to Ghanaians alone.

The lack of knowledge about the time differences accounts for calls at such awkward times when one may be asleep or at work. Invariably, such calls from parents, spouses, children, family members, and friends have monetary undertones. They call for money to pay for school fees, health care, burial and funeral expenses, and, above all, for food. Thus, much pressure is exerted on the immigrants, who must work harder to be able to assist in some of these demands.

In some instances, some of these people reaching out for financial help may have contributed to your upbringing in education or even sponsored your trip abroad. Therefore, you are obliged to reciprocate such a good deed. According to Prof. Miriam Awumbilah, director of the Migrating out of Poverty Project at the Centre for Migration Studies at the University of Ghana, "a research conducted into the relationship between migration and well-being, showed that a significant proportion of household believed that their welfare had improved as a result of migration of a member. The study also showed that migration had also improved assets accumulation of more migrant than non-migrant households" (*Ghanaian Chronicle*, September 24, 2014).

United States

My experience of rural and city lives in both Ghana and America has put me in a position that I can make a fair comparison of life. It has enabled me to erase some misconceptions I had before coming to America. One day I was walking with my oldest daughter, who had recently arrived in Chicago. In the course of our strolling, she saw some homeless people sleeping on the pavement and under bridges while some others were panhandling. Her remark was, "When you are in Ghana, you think anybody in America is a rich person."

An article written by Jason Cox enumerated some of the major causes of homelessness, which include, among other things: "Poverty remains the top cause of homelessness. Other factors include loss of job, debt from medical expenses, mental illness, drug addition, disability, natural disasters – flood, fire, tornadoes" (source: Wikipedia: The Free Encyclopedia).

In another development, I was having a conversation with a Ghanaian lady some time ago, and she said that if she had not come to America she would not have believed that rodents and pests live in America. These two observations epitomize the misconceptions some people have about developed countries. I believe such misconceptions are not limited to Ghanaians alone but similar to people from the developing world who have not had the opportunity to live in America or any of the developed world. It is therefore erroneous for some people to think or believe that there are no poor people in America and, for that matter, the developed world.

In America, the federal government has a program that assists the low-income earners and the poor. This program, which is executed by the state governments, provides subsidies in the areas of housing, medical insurance, and food to those who apply for any of them. In the field of education, there are no public boarding high schools, but the students enjoy free or reduced-fee breakfast and lunch at the elementary schools, depending on the parents' income.

The hard facts are that America is a country with abundant opportunities in educational development, wealth generation, freedom of religious expression, societal improvement, and, above all, personal development. With hard work, dedication, and perseverance while remaining focused, one's aspirations are achievable in advanced countries. On the other hand, if one falls wayward or falls short of the above qualities, one is likely to become a pauper, land in jail, or become a drug addict, which may eventually push one to become homeless or a panhandler as was observed by my daughter.

As education is the key to development, both personal and societal, in the developed nations, through education, the self-service concept is highly encouraged. For instance, at gasoline stations, drivers fill their own tanks with gasoline. In some of the big stores, there are self-checkout systems for easy transactions. With hard work and dedication while remaining focused, one can achieve his ambition in developed nations without any hindrance whatsoever.

With regard to rodents and pests, they are present in any human habitation, but with persistent controls, their spread is always limited in developed countries. Effective pest control mechanisms by professionals can help eradicate them. According to MedicineNet.com, "Unlike cockroaches and fleas that feed on filth, there is often no relationship between bed bugs and cleanliness. Since bed bugs feed solely on blood, pristine dwellings can be vulnerable to infestation as are places of squalor. Immigration and international travel have contributed to the resurgence of bed bugs in the United States."

Many news reports in recent years have focused on the discovery of bedbugs in even upscale hotels, and a number of lawsuits have been filed by guests in these fashionable hotels who awoke to find hundreds of bedbug bites covering their skin. Because bedbugs can arrive on clothing or in the suitcases of guests from infested hotels or homes harboring the pests, hotels can be an easy target for bedbug infestation. In addition to hotels, bedbugs have been found in movie theaters, office buildings, Laundromats, shelters, apartment buildings, schools, transportation vehicles, and other locations where people may congregate.

Poverty, disease, and premature deaths are prevalent in any human society, but in certain societies, especially in developing countries, these misfortunes are mostly attributed to witchcraft and superstition. According to Richard H. Robbins in his book *Cultural Anthropology: A Problem-Based Approach*, fifth edition, page 5:

> Members of some societies accept death as a natural and inevitable occurrence, whereas others always attribute death to the malevolent act of some person, often through sorcery. In these societies, every death elicits suspicion and a demand for vengeance. Members of other societies require great demonstrations of grief and mourning for the deceased.

> This is not an isolated incident as more often than not, old women are accused of witchcraft in some developing countries including Ghana. Superstition is very prevalent in most developing countries, even among some intellectuals, though few, who link every misfortune to some supernatural powers. The existence of evil spirits and evil-minded people cannot be ruled out in the world but such beliefs

must not saturate our thinking to the detriment of our personal and societal development. Religious scriptures enjoin believers to constantly seek Divine protection against all the hidden and manifest evil in the world.

Media Source published a book titled *Too Young to Die: 100+ Deaths That Stunned the World*. In this publication are the recordings of celebrities who were deemed to have died too young, most of them before their fortieth birthday. Though some of these celebrities died as the result of substance abuse or suicide, some were accidental deaths or from a natural cause.

For example, in February 1993 Reggie Lewis was the captain of the Boston Celtics and an all-star in the National Basketball Association (NBA). "Reggie Lewis joined a friend one afternoon to baskets against his doctor's advice. He suddenly crumpled to the floor. Two hours later, the 28-year-old was pronounced dead at the hospital of sudden cardiac death, a structural heart defect considered the most common cause of death in young athletes. Rumors of drug use ensued, but Lewis' autopsy showed no drugs in his system" (source: *Media Source Magazine*, page 77).

In America and other developed countries, causes of sudden deaths are investigated, and strange diseases are thoroughly researched to find an appropriate prevention and possible cure. However, this is not the case in some developing countries. Prevention of diseases through vaccination is more encouraged in the developed world. As an example, the Chicago Public Schools will demand a certificate of immunization from a licensed physician certifying that a child has taken all the required immunizations before admitting the child into any school in the city. In addition to that, the child will have to undergo periodic vision and dental examinations. Also, children in kindergarten are taught the rudiments of personal hygiene by introducing them to proper handwashing with hand soap or hand sanitizer after using the restroom.

In the same vein, disabled people are given the necessary training to become self-supporting and contribute their quota to the development of the country. I am very certain that these procedures are prevalent in developed countries. Unfortunately, such practices are not available in most developing countries. Usually disabled people are left at the mercy of relatives or philanthropists or left to cater for themselves by begging on the streets.

Electricity, Water, and Sanitation

Electricity and water are the two basic necessities of life in any human society. In the United States and other developed countries of the world, these basic necessities are in abundance and therefore pose no problem to the communities. If for some reasons power outages happen, probably as a result of thunderstorm or other natural occurrences, company workers tirelessly work to restore power as quickly as possible. However, in some developing countries, these necessities pose very serious problems that negatively impact the lives of the people for both domestic and industrial usage.

In Ghana, for instance, frequent power outages for more than three years have negatively impacted personal and industrial development. This trend has led to the collapse of a number of businesses, especially cold stores, hair braiders, mechanics, the hospitality industry, and many small businesses that cannot afford the extra cost of generators. Other sensitive areas like hospitals have not been spared. Even those who can purchase generators for domestic use eventually find the use unprofitable because of the cost of fueling them. Any time one calls a family member or a friend in Ghana, most of the conversation will focus on the power outages. The unscheduled power outages have led to stocks of food items going bad, while some operators of small-scale businesses, such as Internet cafés, drinking bars, and restaurants, have closed down. Refrigerators, televisions, and other electrical appliances have been rendered virtually useless, because people without generators cannot use them. The new practice is for people to carry their phone chargers wherever they go with the hope of getting access to a power source.

One institution that has recently experienced the frustrations faced by Ghanaians is the parliament. The Daily Graphic Online News of November 22, 2014, stated that "On Thursday morning when parliament reconvened, the power went off just as the Speaker of Parliament; Mr. Edward Doe Adjaho was saying a prayer for the commencement of the day's business. 'This is the time for us to investigate this. It is unacceptable for us to continue going through this and we will investigate it.' The Honorable Speaker said."

Water

Another disturbing issue is the frequent water shortage. Ghana Web general news on Friday, October, 24, 2014, stated the Ghana Water Company Limited (GWCL) said, "Its operations are being affected by the nationwide load shedding exercise. Anytime there is a general outage, we also have our plants being affected because we don't have power. Our operations are such that, sometimes when the power is shut down for just one hour, we lose all the water that we have in the system" (source: Ghana Web/TV3 network.com).

Sanitation

According to Water and Sanitation for Urban Poor (WSUP), a nongovernmental organization, "With the increasing pace of urbanization in Ghana, city authorities are finding it ever difficult to provide basic water and sanitation services to everyone. Water and Sanitation coverage in Ghana is low (approximately 61% and 40%) respectively and only 19% of Ghana's population has access to an improved source of sanitation" (source: Ghanaweb.com).

In view of the poor sanitation situation in Ghana that caused an outbreak of cholera killing about 150 people, the president of Ghana, John Dramani Mahama, launched National Sanitation Day to sensitize Ghanaians on the need for proper sanitation. At the launching of the first National Sanitation Day, he said, "Fellow Country men and women, we have witnessed severe incidence of cholera in our country, which resulted in a needless death of our compatriots. These annual cycle of cholera outbreaks is linked to insanitary conditions and unacceptable socio-cultural habits, coupled with an infrastructure deficit. These deaths are indeed painful and unacceptable" (source: Ghana Web. General News of November 1, 2014).

Contrary to the poor water and sanitation provision experienced in most developing countries, the developed world embarks on an aggressive water and sanitation program. Good drinking water is a must for every household and establishment for domestic and commercial purposes and can be found in abundance. Good sanitation programs are maintained to rid cities and towns of filth and rodents. For instance, the Chicago Department of Streets and Sanitation is responsible for a variety of functions, including garbage collection, street lamp maintenance, rodent abatement, graffiti removal, and abandoned vehicle towing. It also provides street sweeping with specially designed trucks, snow plowing with snow trucks, and tree planting and trimming services. Furthermore, this department installs and maintains the city's signalized traffic intersections, street and alley lights, as well as electrical and telephone systems.

One of the city's most effective ways to control rodents is

containerization. Residents use heavy-duty plastic bags with tightly fitting lids to contain garbage. By doing this, residents are able to cut off one of the main sources of food in an urban rat's diet. Combined with rodenticide, the city is able to reduce the increase of rats in the city. Any animal carcass found on the public way is removed by the department of streets and sanitation. More than 1.5 million heavy-duty plastic ninety-five-gallon carts with tight lids are supplied free to single-family residences and apartment buildings. These free carts, combined with rodenticide placed deep inside rat burrows, are the key reasons for the decline of rats in the city. Missing or damaged carts are replaced for free. (source: City of Chicago Website)

My Humble Message

The developed countries have gone through a series of teething problems during the formative periods of their development. Some have gone through revolutions and civil wars, while others achieved independence hundreds of years ago. There are others that were never colonized at all. With the developing countries, especially African countries, the majority attained their independence less than fifty years ago and are still undergoing periods of gestation, so it will take some time before some can stand well on their feet.

Through education, science, and technology, the developed nations have made very significant improvements in their economies, health, industry, and much more. These areas of development are now taking place in most developing nations, so the possibility of pitfalls along the way is very high, and that must be taken into consideration by the developed nations. That notwithstanding, leaders of developing countries must make judicious use of the natural resources that their nations have been endowed with for the benefit of all the citizenry, not just the ruling class and the elite in the society. Such social misdeeds as avarice, graft, corruption, nepotism, and favoritism, which are detrimental to societal growth, must be reduced to the barest minimum if they cannot be completely eliminated.

However, irresponsible leadership manifested in unbridled bribery and corruption, as well as nepotism and favoritism in some developing nations have led to these nations lacking basic essential human services for the majority of the population. Such basic services include electricity, good drinking water, good sanitation programs, better schools, good roads, and well-equipped hospitals. These things can be greatly improved with proper planning.

Education needs to be made available to all children in developing nations, especially in Africa. In order to curb illegal migrations, governments must create well-paid jobs that will keep their citizens, especially the youth, in their home countries. It is very disheartening to read, hear, and learn that we lose the best of our youth through illegal migration, and sometimes this leads to death. It is nearly impossible to stop the practice of illegal migration, but the number can be reduced drastically if prudent measures are taken by governments. If those in positions of authority shun greed and selfishness at the expense of the majority of the population, some savings can be made to improve the lives of the majority of the people. With a concerted effort exhibiting a sense of patriotism and nationalism and each individual contributing effectively to national development, developing nations can accelerate their developmental objectives.

Corruption

Corruption as a moral and social ill is not limited to developing nations, but its widespread consequences differ between developed nations and developing countries. In developed countries, corrupt officials and politicians receive the appropriate punishment irrespective of social or political status in the society, which is rather the opposite of what happens in developing nations.

Most developing countries do not take punitive measures against corrupt public officials and politicians, especially when the perpetrator belongs to the ruling party. The keynote address by the former president of Ghana, Flt. Lt. Jerry John Rawlings, on the topic of emerging democracies in Africa, which he gave at a conference organized by the National Institute for Legislative Studies in Abuja, Nigeria, on June 17, 2013, highlights my point. He said in part, "We live in countries where poor, petty thieves get imprisoned for several years while businessmen who evade taxes in millions of dollars or a politician who misappropriates millions of state funds escape punishment."

In another development, an article written by Patrick Vanhulle on August 9, 2009, and broadcast on Deutsche Welle, Germany's international broadcast, was titled "Corrupt Political Elites Block Development in Africa." He quoted from a book written by former German Ambassador Volker Seitz, who spent seventeen years of his diplomatic career between 1965 and 1982 in Africa. In his book, he writes: "Corruption is a big issue in Africa." He claims that the continent has a wealth of natural and human resources but lacks responsible leaders. "The political elites I've met have Europe or the United States on their mind, not their own population."

In another article by Patrick Vanhulle, he referenced the latest book of Moeletsi Mbeki, the younger brother of former South African President, Thabo Mbeki. According to him, "Economic growth figures are looking good in most parts of Africa, but it doesn't mean the standard of living is increasing. A lot of countries are benefitting from prices from raw materials and export goods, but that isn't really dripping down to the general population; the poverty level is fairly stagnant" (source: the World Economic Forum on Africa / Deutsche Welle).

It is my fervent conviction that if developing countries, especially in Africa, embrace education seriously at all levels, thus increasing the literacy rate of the population, it would catapult their developmental aspirations. Governments must struggle to fight such moral and social vices as bribery and corruption the top down; eliminate nepotism, favoritism, and selfishness; and embrace the spirit of patriotism. This must be done in a concerted effort for development to be achievable.

Incomes from natural resources must be geared toward improving the lives of the majority of the people by building such infrastructure as schools, hospitals, affordable housing, and roads just to mention a few things. All of this would be for the benefit of all people. Corrupt officials and those who misappropriate public funds must be punished accordingly, irrespective of status in society or political affiliation. Governments must endeavor to create an enabling environment for economic progress by encouraging and promoting entrepreneurship among the citizens of those countries, as well as aggressive industrialization and mechanized farming. By so doing, youth unemployment can be minimized.

Other Factors

Sometimes, societal developments are hampered by such things as chieftaincy and land disputes that lead to prolonged litigation and may eventually result in poverty. Community and tribal misunderstandings might lead to conflicts, fighting, and, at worst, war. Some of us from developing countries are not accustomed to such simple courtesies as saying please and thank you or giving an instant apology. In certain instances, an elder or a person in authority feels too demeaned to apologize to a younger person or a subordinate. The same is often true with a husband apologizing to his wife.

Before Dr. K.A Busia became the prime minister of Ghana, he

was the chairman for the Center for Civic Education. One of the slogans of the center that I admired most was, "Courtesy pays much but costs nothing." When I began working at O'Hare International Airport, as I was entering the office one day, a black lady who was ahead of me held the door for me to enter. After punching in my time card, she pulled me aside and said, "Sadik, so you could not even say thank you to me?" I felt really embarrassed by her comment, for I did not realize how worried she was by my inaction. I failed to apply etiquette, which include saying please and thank you and showing up on time. These things imply a sign of respect. It's also important to listen to others. When someone speaks to you, you must really pay attention to what is being said without any interruption. Respecting others' privacy is another aspect of etiquette.

My membership in the Ghana National Council, United African Organization, Asanteman Association, and Ghanaian Cab Drivers Association has enabled me to make a lot of friends to Ghanaians and non-Ghanaians alike. People who otherwise would have been unknown to me have now become very good friends—one of the benefits of being social.

While I was attending a social function of Ghanaians in Chicago, I met one of my classmates from T.I. AMASS, George Gorleku Tetteh. He was a very amiable person who was a prominent player on the school's soccer team in the 1960s. It was a very momentous meeting, and we shared memories of our school days. By and by, I met even more past students of T.I. AMASS, some of whom were my former students.

Prospective Travelers

My piece of advice for prospective travelers is that you must be wary of what information you get from some people, because most of what you hear will be half-truths. Some people have the presumption that winning the American Diversity Visa Lottery and receiving a permanent immigrant visa will automatically enable the prospective immigrant get a job and find accommodations in America. This is totally untrue. Obtaining the permanent immigrant visa, popularly known as a green card, only enables the recipient to live in America permanently. Then, after five years, the immigrant can apply for a citizenship status if desired by paying the appropriate fee. The acquisition of a job and accommodation is the immigrant's own problem.

With hard work and perseverance, an immigrant can achieve prosperity in advanced countries, but usually, it is not as easy as we perceive while in the developing country. Some people leave their lucrative jobs at home only to become disappointed in their pursuit of greener pastures. It is not very likely that all such people will get better or similar jobs abroad.

An Indian friend of mine confided in me that he had become greatly disappointed after leaving his lucrative job in Saudi Arabia for America. According to him, he was earning much more money as a truck driver in Saudi Arabia, but when he came to America, because of his limited knowledge in the English language, he had to be content with some menial job receiving far less pay. Though truck driving is a well-paid job in America, but because he could not read or write English, he could not write and pass the examination to obtain a truck license. One has to read extensively to pass the written test before the practical test. This is just one of the many examples of disappointments some immigrants experience in foreign countries. However, such adult immigrants have the consolation that their children can have better opportunities in America and other developed countries.

ABOUT THE AUTHOR

Sadik Bosompem Aboagye Sr. is currently the executive secretary of the Ghana National Council of Metropolitan Chicago, the umbrella organization of the Ghanaian community in Chicago. He has served in various executive positions in the previous administration of the council, as well as the Asanteman Association of Chicago and Midwest. Presently, he is a chauffeur in  Chicago. In his native country of Ghana, he taught in elementary school for six years, from 1973 to 1979, and then in high school for twelve years, from 1985 to 1997. While in Chicago, he worked with Alright Parking for six months. He later worked as a passenger service agent at Chicago's O'Hare International Airport and also as a substitute teacher with Chicago Public Schools for six years from April 2000 to November 2006.

He holds a bachelor's degree in Social Studies Education from the University of Winneba and a diploma certificate in the Study of Religions and Philosophy from the University of Ghana–Legon.

Born in Anyanso, a rural community in the Bosome-Freho District of the Ashanti Region of Ghana, Sadik Bosompem Aboagye attended the T.I Ahmadiyya Secondary School in Kumasi, Ghana. He graduated in 1970 and then studied at the Bagabaga Teacher Training College in Tamale in the northern region of Ghana. He received his professional teacher's certificate in 1973. After teaching in the elementary schools for six years, he gained admission to the University of Ghana–Legon in 1979 for a diploma course in the Study of Religions and Philosophy.

After graduation in 1981, he performed his national service assignment at T.I. AMASS. With a sojourn in Nigeria, he returned to teach at T.I. AMASS in 1985, where he remained till 1997 when he went back to study at the University of Winneba for a degree course in Social Studies Education. At T.I. AMASS, he was the secretary of the school's Parent-Teacher Association until he left the school for further studies in 1997. As a student in Winneba, he won the American Diversity Visa Lottery, which enabled him and his family to migrate to America.

Currently, he lives with his wife, children, and grandchildren in Chicago, Illinois, in the United States of America.

Abdullah Mahmud Sam
Regional Manager
Ahmadiyya Education Unit
Kumasi-Ashanti, Ghana

APPENDIX 1

GHANA: A SYNOPSIS

Overview

I am a native of Ghana, a West African country that is bounded on the south by the Gulf of Guinea, an arm of the Atlantic Ocean. Ghana shares boundaries with the republics of Cote d'Ivoire (formerly Ivory Coast) on the west, Burkina Faso (Upper Volta) on the north, and Togo on the east. Modern Ghana takes its name from the ancient kingdom of Ghana, some five hundred miles to the north of present-day Accra, which flourished until the eleventh century AD.

One of the great Sudanic states that dominated African history, the kingdom of Ghana controlled the gold trade between the mining areas to the south and the Saharan routes to the north. Ancient Ghana was also the focus for the trade in Saharan copper and salt. The coming of the Europeans altered the trading patterns, and the focus of economic power shifted to the West African coastline. In due course, however, slaves replaced gold as the most lucrative trade along the coast with European slave buyers using the forts and the adjoining buildings for their own accommodations and protection, as well as for storing the goods, mainly guns and gunpowder, which they would barter for slaves. Some of the forts were also used for keeping newly acquired slaves pending the arrival of the ships to collect them. The European nations quarreled over access to the coastal lands, and eventually the British won control of the costal trade from the other European nations. It took the British more than fifty years of military campaigns to subdue the Asante Empire to take total control of Ghana.

Meanwhile, Some Ghanaian politicians and intellectuals were yearning for autonomy of the nation by the formation of the United Gold Coast Convention (UGCC), a political party. Leaders of the party were Ebenezer Ako-Adjei, Edward Akuffo-Addo, Joseph Boakye Danquah, Emmanuel Obetsebi-Lamptey, and William Ofori-Attah. The UGCC invited Kwame Nkrumah to return from Britain to Ghana as the general secretary of the party. The six nationalists thereafter became known as the Big Six in Ghana's political history. The man who was the catalyst of that struggle was Dr. Kwame Nkrumah.

Born in 1909, Dr. Nkrumah trained as a teacher at Achimota College in Ghana and then the United States and Britain, where he obtained his degrees. He became prominent as a leader of West African students' organization in London. There he met such personalities as Marcus Garvey and W.E.B. Dubois. He was invited to return to Ghana as the general secretary of the UGCC. In 1949 he broke away from the party and formed Convention People's Party, with the slogan Self-Government Now. In February 1951 his party became victorious in the national pools, and he became the leader of government business.

Osagyefo Dr. Kwame Nkrumah led Ghana to achieve Independence from the British colonial government in 1957, the first African country south of the Sahara to get out of the colonial rule. In 2000 Nkrumah was voted Africa's man of the millennium by the listeners to the British Broadcasting Corporation (BBC) World Service Program, being described by the BBC as a "Hero of Independence, an International Symbol of freedom as the leader of the first black African country to shake off the chains of colonial rule" (source: "Kwame Nkrumah's Vision of Africa," BBC World Service, September 14, 2000).

As midnight struck, on March 5, 1957, and Gold Coast became Ghana, Nkrumah declared, "We are going to see that we create our own African personality and identity, we again rededicate ourselves in the struggle to emancipate other countries in Africa; for our independence is meaningless unless it is linked up with the total liberation of the African continent" (source: http://nkrumahinfobank.org/).

In 1960 Ghana became a republic, and Nkrumah declared Ghana a one-party system of government. Nkrumah ruled Ghana until his government was overthrown by a military and police coup d'état on February 24, 1966.

Brief Political Development

The architects of the plot that overthrew Nkrumah and his Convention Peoples Party (CPP) were Maj. E. K. Kotoka and Col. Akwasi Amankwaa Afrifa. The military constituted the National Liberation Council (NLC) headed by Lt. Gen. Joseph Arthur Ankrah. In April 1969 Lt. Gen. Akwasi Amankwa Afrifa became the chairman of a three-man presidential commission. Ghana entered into the second republic in 1969 as a multiparty democracy. The party in power was the Progress Party with Dr. Kofi Abrefa Busia as the prime minister and leader of government. Justice Edward Akuffo Addo became the president. That government was also overthrown by the military on January 13, 1972. The leaders constituted the Supreme Military Council (SMC) composed of senior military officers led by Ignatius Kutu Acheampong.

In 1978 there was a palace coup to restructure the government with Frederick W.K. Akuffo as the head of the SMC II. The SMC II government ruled from July 5, 1978, to June 4, 1979, when young military officers led by Flt. Lt. Jerry John Rawlings overthrew the SMC II government. The young officers constituted the Armed Forces Revolutionary Council (AFRC). The AFRC, in a move to purge the military of corruption, executed eight military officers, three of whom were former heads of state. From June to September 1979, special courts held hearings and sentenced 155 military officers, former officials, and wealthy businessmen to prison terms ranging from six months to ninety-five years. (source: the Library of Congress Country Studies; CIA World fact book / Ghana Web)

As a first step in the housecleaning exercise, former head of state Gen. I.K. Acheampong and Maj. Gen. E.K. Utuka were executed by firing squad at the Teshi military range on June 16, 1979, after a hastily assembled revolutionary court. Ten days later, on June 26, the death sentence was announced for former heads of state Gen. F.W.K. Akuffo and Lt. Gen. A.A. Afrifa, as well as Maj. Gen. R.E.A. Kotei, Air Vice-Marshall George Yaw Boakye, Real Adm. J.K. Amedume, and Col. R.J.A Felli.

The country was ushered into the third republic later in September 24, 1979, in a multiparty democracy. Dr. Hilla Liman of the People's National Party was the president. The third republic also fell on December 31, 1979, in another Rawlings-led coup. Rawlings then became the head of state in the government of the Provisional National Defence Council. Ghana returned to fourth constitutional democratic government, which was inaugurated on January 7, 1993. Jerry John Rawlings's National Democratic Congress (NDC) won the elections. However, fraud allegations led to an electoral boycott by the main opposition party, the New Patriotic Party (NPP), resulting in an effective one-party system with the NDC.

In the 2000 general elections, the opposition NPP won the elections, and John Agyekum Kuffour became the president. He ruled for two terms of eight years, but the opposition NDC regained the control of government in the 2008 general elections with Prof. John Evans Atta Mills as the president. President Mills died on July 24, 2012, while in office, and Vice President John Dramani Mahama completed his term of office. However, John Dramani Mahama won the general elections in 2012 and is currently the president of the Republic of Ghana.

Climate and Vegetation

The climate of Ghana is tropical, but temperatures vary depending on the season and elevation. There are two main seasons in Ghana: the wet or rainy season and the dry season. The northern part of Ghana experiences its rainy season from March to November, while the south experiences its rainy season from April to mid-November. The average annual rainfall ranges from about forty-three inches in the northern parts to about eighty-three inches in the southern parts of the country. The harmattan, a dry desert wind, blows from the northeast from December to March, lowering the humidity and creating hot days and cool nights. In the south the effects of the harmattan are felt in January. The average annual temperature in Ghana is about 79°F (26°C).

Ghana is generally a lowland country except for a range of hills on the eastern border. Southern Ghana consists of evergreen, semideciduous forests with such valuable trees as mahogany, odum, and ebony. Northern Ghana, which occupies about two-thirds of the country, is covered by savanna grassland with scattered trees and shrubs. Much of the natural vegetation of Ghana has been destroyed by land clearing for agriculture, illegal logging, and other related activities. Once plentiful throughout the savanna, large mammals such as elephants and lions are now very rare and largely confined to the nature reserves. Periodic drought and deforestation have led to the desertification and soil erosion. Ghana has the largest man-made lake in the world, the Volta Lake.

Economy

Ghana's economy is dominated by agriculture, which employs about 60 percent of the working population in the production of both cash and food crops. Ghana is the third largest producer of cocoa in the world. In addition to cocoa, Ghana has other natural resources, including gold, diamonds, timber, bauxite, and manganese. Oil was found in 2007.

Tourism also generates some income for the country. Tourism attractions include Mole National Park, Kakum National Park, Lake Bosomtwe, Volta Lake, Paga Crocodile Pond, Bunso Arboretum, Bobri Butterfly Sanctuary, Salaga slave market, Cape-Coast Castle, Elmina Castle, and Shai Hills Resource Reserve. Ghana also relies heavily on foreign assistance and remittances from Ghanaians abroad.

Appendix 2

Chicago

Brief History

According to DePaul Center for Urban Education, Chicago has played an important role in the history of the United States. Located in the center of the United States on the shores of Lake Michigan, Chicago has become a vibrant world-class city that is rich in history. According to explorers' accounts from the 1600s, the Illinois Indians were the first people to claim a land they named *Chicaugou*, which meant strong or great and was used by many tribal chiefs to signify that they were great chiefs. Other accounts suggest that the meaning of *Che-cau-gou* comes from the strong-smelling onions that grew there.

The first explorers to set foot on the site destined to become Chicago were Louis Joliet and Fr. Jacques Marquette. The two explorers were commissioned by the French government in 1673. Father Marquette returned to the area one year later to establish an Indian mission.

Chicago's first permanent settler, Jean Baptiste Point du Sable was a Haitian trapper. He and his Indian wife came to the area in

1780. Point du Sable came to America as a young man after going to school in Paris, France. Point du Sable built a trading post in the wilderness and traded in furs with the Indians on the north bank of Chicago River. He lived with his wife, Catherine, until 1796. More and more people came to live at the trading post, which, ultimately, became the city of Chicago. He later moved with his wife to settle in Peoria, Illinois. The completion of Illinois-Michigan canal in 1848, which joined the Chicago River with the Mississippi River, coupled with the arrival of the first locomotives, positioned Chicago to become the crossroads of the nation.

Though Chicago suffered a series of setbacks, including the Fort Dearborn Massacre by a tribe of hostile Indians, and the War of 1812 between the United States and Great Britain, it was able to maintain its territorial possessions and expand its boundaries. In 1837 Chicago was incorporated as a city with a population of 4,170, covering an area of 10 square miles. The borders were North Avenue on the north, Cermak on the south, Michigan Avenue on the east, and Wood Street on the west.

With the development of the railroad and the Illinois and Michigan Canal, Chicago advanced as the leader in the cattle, hog, lumber, and wheat industries. By 1850, the population had increased to 29,963, with more than 50 percent being immigrants from England, Wales, Germany, France, and Ireland.

Word spread that the city was full of opportunities, and by the mid-1850s, as many as one hundred thousand immigrants flocked to the city annually, seeking land and jobs. In 1860 Chicago hosted the Republican National Convention that nominated Illinois' own Abraham Lincoln as the presidential candidate. Lincoln won the elections to become the sixteenth president of the United States of America. One year later, the Civil War began. Post–Civil War America saw Chicago growing in population; grain shipment doubled, and merchants prospered.

In October 1871, the Great Chicago Fire destroyed most of the city's central area. It started in the lumber district on the west side of the city. It is said that Mrs. O'Leary's cow allegedly knocked over a kerosene lamp that started the fire. The fire destroyed nearly four square miles of the city, claimed at least 250 lives, and left about 100,000 residents homeless. More than 17,000 buildings were destroyed, and property damage was estimated at about $200 million. The debris from the fire was pushed into the lake, making a landfill for much of the present downtown lakefront.

Chicago is basically divided into three parts: the north side, the south side, and the west side. The east is bordered by Lake Michigan, but it gradually widens southward from North Avenue (1600 North) through the southeast part of the city. Chicago remains highly segregated by race and economics. The north side is predominantly white and affluent, the west side is more Hispanic, and the south side is wholly black or African American and mostly poorer.

After the fire, the greater Chicago emerged. Internationally acclaimed architects flocked to the city for its reconstruction. Chicago was thus resurrected. In 1871 a tunnel was constructed under the Chicago River at LaSalle Street. By 1884, the population had increased to 629,985. In 1885 the world's first skyscraper was built in Chicago, the first elevated train was built in Chicago in 1892, and the first subway built in Chicago in 1938. (source: Ibid)

The first half of the twentieth century saw the arrival of hundreds of thousands of African Americans from the South, who, like newcomers from across the Atlantic, came to escape political oppression and economic deprivation. The second half of the twentieth century brought a new wave of immigrants to Chicago, primarily from Spanish-speaking countries, especially Mexico. Today, Chicago is a dynamic and culturally diverse city. It is an international center for business and leisure travel, due in part to the city's transportation accessibility, a thriving business community, world-class hotels, restaurants, shopping, arts, and entertainment.

Chicago Neighborhoods

Chicago has seventy-seven distinct neighborhoods, some of which are worth mentioning.

The Loop is the city's financial and political hub, which mixes plenty of play with work. From top cultural institutions and live theater district to sprawling parks, major shopping, and the nation's most famous architecture, the Loop is the heart of downtown Chicago. South of the Chicago River on the north and west, Lake Michigan on the east, and Roosevelt Road to the south, the area has been referred to as the Loop since the 1880s. The area still carries on the transportation tradition with the iconic L rail tracks that circle overhead. Like much of the city, most Loop structures were destroyed in the 1871 Chicago fire, but the city's can-do attitude inspired subsequent innovations in building designs that led to the country's earlier skyscrapers, many of which are still a dynamic part of the Loop. Major structures include Daley Center, Chicago Board of Trade, Grant Park, Buckingham Fountain, Goodman Theater, Chicago Theater, Chicago Cultural Center, Museum Campus, Art Institute of Chicago, and Harold Washington Library.

South Loop encompasses the Burnham Park and Printer's Row and is bounded by Congress Parkway and Polk Street. Once, the center of Chicago's printing industry, today Printer's Row bustles with bookstores, restaurants, and residential lofts that were converted from former warehouses.

Old Town is bounded by Armitage Street on the north, Oak Street on the south, Clark Street on the east, and Halsted

Street on the west. Many of the streets in Old Town predate the Great Chicago Fire of 1871. The first nonnative settlers were German immigrants in the 1850s. Famed Second City Theater and Steppenwolf are located in this community in addition to some bars and restaurants.

Gold Coast is one of the most affluent neighborhoods in the nation. Gold Coast lends itself to leisurely walks along the tree-lined streets, one of which is the Astor Street.

Magnificent Mile stretches along Michigan Avenue from Oak Street north to the Chicago River on the south. Cultural gems include the Museum of Contemporary Art, Loyola University (Downtown Campus), Wrigley Building, Tribune Tower, and the historic Water Tower Place, one of the only buildings to survive the Great Chicago Fire. The Magnificent Mile is home to many shopping stores along Michigan Avenue and a number of hotels and eateries. It is, therefore, not surprising that vehicular and human traffic abound in this neighborhood, especially those traveling to festive occasions.

The River North neighborhood is bounded by Chicago Avenue on the north, Chicago River on the south, Michigan Avenue on the east, and Orleans Street on the west. Named for its proximity to the Chicago River, this neighborhood has undergone several changes in its history. Previously an industrial area, it can now boast of a cluster of high-rise condominiums, a large concentration of bars and restaurants, and art galleries. The legendary Merchandise Mart, which houses the world's largest collection of home furnishing showrooms, is also located in this neighborhood.

Lincoln Park is bordered by Lake Michigan on the east, Chicago River on the west, North Avenue on the south, and Diversey Parkway on the north. Like much of Chicago, Lincoln Park was originally a swampy and grassy suburb that was later annexed to the city. The first wave of European immigrants was made up of Germans. The second largest influx included both Scottish and Irish immigrants.

Lake View neighborhood is bordered by Lake Michigan on the east, Ashland Avenue on the west, Diversey Parkway on the south, and Irving Park Road on the north. This neighborhood is also the home of German, Irish, and Scottish immigrants. The famed Wrigley Field, the home of the Chicago Cubs baseball team, is in this locality. A lot of bars and restaurants abound in this area. Nightlife, especially on weekends, is very exciting. Very particular with this neighborhood is Boystown, where gay bars and funky shops are the norm. The annual gay and lesbians parade takes place in this neighborhood when thousands of people from across the country and elsewhere attend. This annual event attracts about a million adherents and spectators.

Bucktown/Wicker Park is a mixed neighborhood of immigrants that center on the streets of Milwaukee, Damen, and North Avenue, creating a vibrant atmosphere. This exciting neighborhood has a lot of boutiques, coffee houses, restaurants, nightclubs, storefronts, and theaters.

Chinatown is a relatively small community surrounding Cermak Road and Wentworth Avenue. A small group of Chinese immigrants landed in Chicago after the completion of the transcontinental railroad in 1869, but in 1970, families fleeing Chinese Communist law boosted the city's Chinese population to about 14,000. The population has since more than tripled.

Little Italy is the oldest continuously Italian neighborhood, and older and younger generations of Tuscans and Sicilians still speak Italian. Family-owned restaurants serve up an authentic taste of Italy.

Pilsen neighborhood is situated on the southwest corner of the Loop. It was named for a city in Bohemia (now part of Czech

Republic) by the immigrants who settled there after the Great Chicago Fire. Mexican immigrants, however, have replaced the Eastern Europeans. Today, Pilsen's Little Village area is known as the best place in Chicago to find true Mexican cooking.

Ukrainian Village, situated west of downtown, is bounded by Division Street on the north, Grand Avenue on the south, Damen Avenue on the east, and Western Avenue on the west. Historically settled by Ukrainians, this is a rich area known for its Byzantine-style churches and beautiful Victorian housing. This was an abode of wealthy German merchants but is currently a mixed neighborhood.

Bridgeport, a south-side neighborhood, is home to the Irish immigrants, whereas Jefferson Park and Portage Park are home to many Polish immigrants who have settled in this northwest neighborhood.

Hyde Park is a south-side neighborhood housing the University of Chicago. It is a mixed community of students, professors, and local residents who are predominantly black.

Overview

Chicago's rich and diverse culture is celebrated across the city. Cultural festivals attract the young and old to neighborhoods founded by the generation of immigrants who built their homes there. The city is home to twenty-six ethnic groups, and Chicagoans collectively speak more than one hundred ethnic languages. Chicago is home to more than fifty skyscrapers and a lot more superstructures, Bascule bridges, and historic sites with the Chicago River running through the city. Chicago has more than five hundred recreational parks of varying sizes, as well as twenty-nine miles of lakefront. (source: *Newcomer's Handbook*)

Chicago is the third largest and most populous city in the

United States with a population of about 3 million. It is situated in the State of Illinois, in the Midwest region of the United States. The 2010 census recorded the actual population as 2,695,598, showing a decline of 200,418, or 6.92 percent. The decline cuts across all the segments of the population. The 2000 population census was 2,896,016.

The main components of the population are whites, blacks or African Americans, Hispanics or Latinos, and others. The whites alone account for 1,212.835, representing 44.99 percent; blacks or African Americans 887,608, representing 32.93 percent; Hispanics or Latino origin account for 778,862, making up for 28.89 percent; and some other race alone account for 360,493, an equivalent of 13.37 percent. In gender population, males account for 1,308,072, a percentage of 48.53, and female population is 1,387,526, which is 51.47 percent. (source: census viewer.com)

Chicago Mayor Rahm Emanuel was elected in 2011 and is the first Jewish mayor and the fifty-fifth mayor of Chicago. He succeeded Mayor Richard M. Daley, the longest serving mayor, who was in office from 1989 to 2011. Mayor Richard M. Daley is the son of former Mayor Richard J. Daley, who served between 1955 and 1976. He died in office. The only female mayor on record was Jane Margaret Byrne, who served from 1979 to 1983. Mayor Harold Washington was the first black/African American mayor and was elected in 1983 but died in office during his second term in 1987. The City Council elected Eugene Sawyer in 1987 to complete Washington's term.

The mayor of Chicago is the chief executive of the City of Chicago. He appoints the commissioners of the Chicago Fire Department, Chicago Police Department, and other heads of Chicago City departments. He also appoints heads of Chicago Public Schools, Chicago Park District, Chicago Public Library, Chicago Housing Authority, and Chicago Transit Authority

(CTA), as well as board members of the various specialized governmental bodies.

The city clerk and city treasurer are elected separately, as are the fifty aldermen who form the city council. The mayor is empowered, however, to fill any vacancies in any of the fifty-two elected offices by appointment. In turn, the city council elects one of its own to fill a mayoral vacancy. The mayor of Chicago is elected by popular vote every four years on the last Tuesday in February. A runoff election is held on the first Tuesday in April in the event no candidate garners more than 50 percent of the vote. Chicago is the largest city in the United States that does not limit the term of service for its mayor. (source: Wikipedia: The Free Encyclopedia)

Chicago abounds in a lot of tourist attractions. Millennium Park, one of Chicago's most popular attractions, includes the reflective sculpture Cloud Gate, better known as The Bean, as well as the Frank Gehry-designed Pritzker Pavilion and the steel ribbon bridge among others. John Hancock Observatory is rated the best view in the city by the *Chicago Tribune*. The ninety-fourth floor observatory, more than one thousand feet above the Magnificent Mile, features the Lavazza Expression Café and 360-degree views. The Willis Tower (formerly Sears Tower) skydeck, 1,353 feet above sea level, offers views through a glass balcony on the 103rd floor. Navy Pier houses more than fifty acres of shops, restaurants, rides, and attractions, including Chicago Children's Museum where kids and families enjoy hands-on exhibits and learning activities, IMAX Theater, and a 150-foot Ferris wheel.

Other tourist attractions include the Museum of Science and Industry, the largest science museum in the Western hemisphere. It exhibits more than three hundred artifacts of historical importance. The DuSable Museum is dedicated to the study of the history and culture of Africans and Americans of African descent. The Harold

Washington Library Center is the largest municipal library in the world, and there's also the Art Institute of Chicago, the Museum of Contemporary Art. The Chicago Cultural Center, housed in a Chicago landmark building, is a cultural gem offering free public events and information programs showcasing live music and visual arts. The Chicago History Museum is a research center devoted to Chicago and American history.

The Museum Campus houses the Shedd Aquarium, Field Museum, and Adler Planetarium, the Midwest's leading museum for astronomy and space imagination. At the famous Millennium Park adjacent Grant Park, visitors can have the fun of the Crown Fountain, a shallow reflecting pool bookended by fifty-foot towers with faces of Chicago citizens projected on LED screens. At the same place, visitors can have a look at the mind-bending photo at the 110-ton Cloud Gate (The Bean).

Across the other side of the Columbus Drive at Grant Park lies the great Buckingham Fountain. The elaborately carved Georgia-marble fountain shoots a geyser spectacle 150 feet in the air every hour beginning at nine o'clock in the morning and illuminates each evening with a light and music show, weather permitting. During the summer seasons, Chicagoans experience a lot of festivities. The various neighborhood food festivals make the city livelier. Prominent among them is the renowned Taste of Chicago, which treats both local and foreign cuisines. (source: This week in Chicago)

Ghanaians are not left out in the summer festivities. The various Ghanaian associations and church organizations organize picnics at different dates and locations. The most important Ghanaian festival is the GhanaFest, which attracts both Ghanaians and non-Ghanaians. Many Ghanaians from around the world visit Chicago to participate in this festival, which has been acclaimed as the biggest cultural exposition of Ghanaians in the diaspora.

Chicago has a large Irish population; as such, Irish culture finds expression in the city. Prominent among those cultures is the celebration of St. Patrick's Day. On that day, the Chicago River is dyed green. Many of the celebrants wear green attire, necklaces, hats, and bands to reflect the Irish national color.

Chicago's summer activities are filled with music festivals, which include Lollapalooza, one of the world's premier music festivals, covering three days of music. With more than one hundred bands and seven stages, the festival takes place at Grant Park. Others include Chicago Gospel Music Festival, Chicago Symphony Orchestra, Chicago Blues Festival, Chicago Jazz Festival, Charter One Pavilion (which provides live concert entertainment), and a host of others.

One of the most important holidays in America is Thanksgiving. Thanksgiving Day is a national holiday celebrated in the United States and Canada as a day of giving thanks for the blessing of the harvest and of the preceding year. It is celebrated on the fourth Thursday of November in the United States and on the second Monday of October in Canada. Thanksgiving has its historical roots in religious and cultural traditions and has long been celebrated in a secular manner as well. The original 1621 feast and time of thanksgiving in Plymouth was prompted by a good harvest. Pilgrims and Puritans who began emigrating from England in the 1620s and 1630s carried the tradition of fasting and thanksgiving with them to New England. New England is a region of the Northeastern United States consisting of the six states of Connecticut, Maine, Massachusetts, New Hampshire, Rhode Island, and Vermont.

It is a day for Americans to come together around the table, a day of family reunion, feasting, game playing, entertainment, and church services.

Chicago preserves the beauty of its beach playgrounds, leaving miles of sandy, sun-soaked fun. Notable among the beaches are North Avenue Beach, Oak Street Beach, Montrose Beach, Foster Avenue Beach, Ohio Street Beach, and Thirty-First Street Beach. Among summer entertainment is the Daredevil Airshow where parachute teams fall in unison from 12,500 feet in the air. Boat teams also display their skills on Lake Michigan. People troop to the various beaches to cool themselves when the temperature is high, and boat owners sail on the Lake Michigan for leisure. (source: Choose Chicago – Official Visitors Guide)

Chicago is home to a number of skyscrapers. Notable among them are Willis Tower (formerly the Sears Tower), which used to be the tallest building in the world until it was overtaken by the Petronas Towers in Kuala Lumpur, Malaysia, in 1998.

Currently, the tallest buildings in the world are as follows: Burj Khalifa or the Dubai Tower in United Arab Emirates (UAE). It was built in 2010 with a height of 2,717 feet. The Makkah Royal Clock Tower Hotel in Mecca, Saudi Arabia, was built in 2012 with a height of 1,971 feet. Taipei 101 Tower in Taipei, Taiwan, was built in 2004 with a height of 1,670 feet. The Shangal World Financial Center in Shangal, China, was built in 2008 with a height of 1,614 feet. International Commerce Center (ICC) in Hong Kong, China, was built in 2010 and has a height of 1,588 feet. The Petronas Towers in Kuala Lumpur, Malaysia, was built in 1998 and has a height of 1,483 feet. The Zifeng Tower (Nanjing Greenland Financial Center) in Nanjing, China, was built in 2009 and has a height of 1,476 feet. The Willis Tower in Chicago has a height of 1,450 feet and was completed in 1974. The Kingkey Finance Center Plaza in Shenzhen, China, was completed in 2011 and has a height of 1,449 feet. The Guangzhou International Finance Center in Guangzhou, China, was completed in 2010 and has a height of 1,440 feet. Trump International Hotel and Tower was completed in 2009 and has a height of 1,389 feet.

One World Trade Center (Freedom Tower) in New York was completed in 2013 and has a height of 1,368 feet. (source: About. com Architecture)

Of the ten tallest buildings in the United States, four are located in Chicago. The Willis Tower is second to One World Trade Center in New York, which was completed on May 10, 2013. The ten tallest buildings in Chicago include Willis Tower, constructed in 1974 with 108 floors; John Hancock Center, built in 1969 with 100 floors; Trump International Hotel and Tower, built in 2009 with 96 floors; and A.O.N. Center, built in 1973 with 83 floors. Others include the Aqua Tower located at 225 N. Columbus Avenue, which was constructed in 2009 with 82 floors; Water Tower Place, which was built in 1976 with 74 floors; Legacy Towers, built in 2010 with 73 floors; Lake Point Tower, built in 1968 with 70 floors; and a host of others having between 50 and 70 floors.

Chicago is one of the most beautiful cities in the world. Its beauty is at its best during the night when the millions of lights illuminate the city's skyscrapers and superstructures, providing a glittering panoramic view. The skyscrapers and the superstructures in downtown Chicago offer ample shade below, so people walking and biking beneath them, especially in the Loop, do not feel the heat from the sun's rays, no matter the intensity. In the other neighborhoods, the numerous trees also give enough shade to pedestrians and bikers alike. During the summer season, service industries such as transportation, hospitality, and restaurants have a booming business. Chicago has awesome summer conditions but awful winter conditions.

Another fascinating event associated with Chicago summer activities is the Chicago Marathon sponsored by Bank of America. The thirty-sixth annual Chicago Marathon took place on Sunday, October 13, 2013, at Chicago's Grant Park. According to *Chicago*

Sun-Times of Monday, October 14, 2013, "This year, about 45,000 marathoners registered, and organizers said 40,230 crossed the starting line, up 2,000 from last year. Race staff said 39,115 finished the race Sunday, topping the record of 37,475 last year. The competition attracted athletes from 13 countries."

Weather Conditions

Chicago falls into the doldrums during the winter season with the cold and freezing conditions. The *Chicago Sun-Times* newspaper of January 7, 2014, carried this headline: "Record-breaking cold disrupts commutes, keep schools closed for another day. As temperatures at O'Hare Airport hit 16 below zero at 7:51 in the morning, and wind chills dropped to minus 42 degrees Fahrenheit, Metra trains were plagued by ice-coated switches. Riders experienced cancellations and nearly two-hour delays." In the same issue, it was reported that "snow depth at O'Hare was 11 inches, and some 1,600 O'Hare flights were canceled through 8:30 pm. Monday, with delays averaging 90 minutes. Midway airport canceled 85 flights and reported delays of up to two hours."

During such very cold temperatures, some people put on layers of clothing, especially those who have to work in the open or walk for some distance. Businesses slow down, and visitors to the city are reduced to the barest minimum. Continuous snowfall and the related potholes make driving very difficult, especially for taxi drivers who have to take their passengers to their doorsteps. Sometimes it's wise to put a shovel in the trunk of the car to scoop out the hardened snow in case you got stuck in it. Usually, if you park your car outside and it snows heavily, you will need to scoop away the snow before you can move your car. During that period, the surfaces of the Chicago River and Lake Michigan become icy. Equally, the grassy parks and flowers that beautify the city become covered with snow. The snow is washed away when the rain comes during the spring season.

The roads become icy and very slippery, causing a number of accidents. During the winter of 2011, severe winter conditions caused a blizzard one day, and some motorists were trapped on expressways and had to be rescued by the security personnel. "A winter blizzard of historic proportions wobbled an otherwise snow-tough Chicago, stranding hundreds of drivers for up to 12 hours overnight on Wednesday, February 2, 2011. The blizzard hammered the city on the first two days of February, dumping more than 20 inches of snow in just 24 hours. The storm forced hundreds of people who became stuck on Lakeshore Drive to abandon their vehicles" (source: Accuweather.com).

During the winter, sometimes the temperature falls below zero degrees Fahrenheit, schools close down. Some people have to put on layers of clothes to battle the weather. But all in all, Chicago, with such nicknames as the Windy City, Second City, City of Big Shoulder, is a great city to live in, notwithstanding the severe cold weather conditions.

Educational Facilities

Chicago, a city with a population of about of 3 million, can boast of seven city colleges for postsecondary education: Harold Washington College, Harry Truman College, Kennedy-King College, Malcolm X College, Olive Harvey College, Wilbur Wright College, and Richard Daley College. All of these are public colleges, which are in addition to the many private colleges offering postsecondary courses. These institutions offer college certificates and associate degrees. Graduates can transfer their credits to a university.

The public universities include, among others, University of Illinois at Chicago, Roosevelt University, Northern Illinois University, Northeastern University, University of Chicago, Chicago State University, Illinois Institute of Art, School of Art Institute of Chicago, Eastern Illinois University, and Governors State University. In addition to these public universities are many more private universities.

Conversely, Ghana, a country with a population of about 25 million, has five public universities: University of Ghana–Legon, University of Science and Technology-Kumasi, University of Development Studies Tamale, University of Cape Coast, University of Winneba, and a few newly established private universities. In addition, Ghana has about thirty-eight postsecondary colleges and polytechnics. It is therefore not surprising that some qualified applicants have to wait for two or more years before they can gain admission to these limited universities.

Sometimes as I watch television and see the city colleges of Chicago and other universities advertise to lure prospective students to their institutions, it saddens me. In Ghana some qualified applicants have to wait for two or more years to gain admission to the universities because of inadequate facilities. At the 2013 congregation ceremony of the University of Ghana, the vice chancellor, Prof. Ernest Ayertey, expressed frustration that "the university was faced with the painful decision of having to turn down the applications of many otherwise well qualified applicants due to limitations of staff and facilities. He disclosed that the University received 52,202 undergraduate and sub-graduate applications out of which the University could only admit 14,695 applicants into the main campuses" (*Daily Graphic*, November 11, 2013).

This is just one aspect of the educational opportunities that exist in America compared to the educational facilities in Ghana.

Most students in postsecondary institutions and universities in the developed world have jobs, at least to cater for their basic needs. However, in most developing countries, this is not possible. The majority of such students have to depend on their parents and relatives for their upkeep and basic needs. Even those who have completed their studies at a university find it very difficult to get employment.

Transportation

Chicago has a very good public transportation system. The city can boast of six interstate highways passing through it, providing efficient and effective public and private transportation to other states and cities. In addition to the road transportation, the railway system is very effective. Furthermore, train and bus services to and from the city to the suburbs are equally efficient.

The Chicago Transit Authority (CTA) provides intracity bus and train services, some of which operate twenty-four hours a day. To make transportation easily accessible and affordable to commuters, bus stops are located at every train station. Bicycle riding is also an integral part of the transportation system in the city.

Chicago has two airports, O'Hare International Airport and Midway International Airport. O'Hare International Airport used to be the busiest airport in the world but has been overtaken by Atlanta's Hartsfield International Airport for that position. According to the Airports Council International (ACI), the world's busiest airports by passenger traffic are measured by total passengers enplaned plus passengers deplaned in addition to direct transit passengers. With reference to the 2013 statistics, Hartsfield-Jackson Atlanta International Airport has been the world's busiest airport since the year 2000, with all airports combined. Of the ten world's busiest airports, four are located in the United States.

The world's busiest airports include:

- Hartsfield-Jackson Atlanta International Airport, Atlanta, Georgia, United States. Total passengers: 94,430,785
- Beijing Capital International Airport, Chaoyang, Beijing, China. Total passengers: 83,712,355
- Heathrow Airport, Hillingdon, London, United Kingdom. Total passengers: 72,368,030
- Tokyo International Airport, Ota, Tokyo, Japan. Total passengers: 68,906,636
- O'Hare International Airport, Chicago, Illinois, United States. Total passengers: 66,883,271
- Los Angeles International Airport, Los Angeles, California, United States. Total passengers: 66,702,252
- Dubai International Airport, Garhound, Dubai, United Arab Emirates. Total passengers: 66,431,533
- Paris Charles de Gaule Airport, Roissy-en-France, France. Total passengers: 62,052,917
- Dallas/Fort Worth International Airport, Dallas/Fort Worth, Texas, United States. Total passengers: 60,436,266
- Soekamo-Hatta International Airport, Cengkaren, Tangerangi-Banten, Indonesia. Total passengers: 59,701,543

In 1949 the Chicago City Council renamed Orchard Field as Chicago O'Hare International Airport to honor the naval aviator Lt. Commander Edward H. "Butch" O'Hare, a Medal of Honor recipient from Chicago who died in World War II. In 1960 an eight-lane expressway opened between O'Hare and downtown Chicago, making the airport more accessible to travelers. In 1984 CTA extended the Blue Line rail service to O'Hare International Airport, which made commuting to the airport fast, easy, and inexpensive. The Airport Transit System (ATS) opened in 1993 to improve the intraterminal passenger transit.

Crime

Like any other big city in America and elsewhere, Chicago has its fair share of gun violence. The *Chicago Sun Times* newspaper of Tuesday, July 8, 2014, reported: "13 killed and at least 58 wounded in shootings across the City during the July 4 2014 Independence holiday weekend." Usually, most of these shootings are gang related, while a few of them are accidental. In many instances, they occur predominantly in certain neighborhoods.

APPENDIX 3

---•◆•---

MY PERCEPTION OF
IMMIGRATION

Migration

Migration is a natural phenomenon in any human society. People migrate from one country to another due to multifarious reasons. Some of the reasons include economic reasons, marriage, political and religious persecutions, conflicts and wars, and the pursuit of freedom. In ancient ages, the modes of migration were by walking and riding on horses and camels. With the advent of boats and ships, traveling to other parts of the world was made easier, so people could travel to faraway places for exploration and trade. Science and technology have made traveling much easier and faster with the invention of automobiles and airplanes. International trade and relations have improved greatly as a result of easier commuting from one nation to another, thus enhancing understanding of the human race.

According to Leah Adams and Anna Kirova in their book, *Global Migration and Education*, "In general, although the term immigrants, migrants and new comers are used differently in other parts of the world, they typically refer to people who have left their places of birth by choice to settle in a new place either permanently or temporarily. The term used to describe the people who have left their homes not by choice are refugees, asylum seekers and displaced people."

Prominent among the reasons for migration is the economic factor. Usually people from poorer countries migrate to richer countries for the achievement of better lives. In addition to enhancing their personal development, these immigrants make enormous contributions to the overall development of the host country.

"Migration of skilled workers is often referred to as a brain drain, and some of the world's poorest countries have the highest incidence of this phenomenon. More than 50% of the university educated professionals from many countries in Central America and the Carribeans live abroad; for some countries this statistics is as higher as 80%. Most college-educated emigrants from developing countries go to the United States, the European Union, Australia and Canada. However, educated migrants often fail to find work that matches their education levels; one of the reasons is lack of frequency in the host language. The family may struggle to obtain enough income for basic necessities, and many new arrivals feel obliged to support family members in their home country. Although the question arises as to whether the brain drain has adverse effects on the sending nation, a World Bank Report (Schiff & Ozden, 2005) clearly shows that the remittances from migrants do help alleviate poverty in the home country" (source: Ibid).

Atlanta Mayor Kasim Reed had this to say about immigration: "The contributions of immigrants and foreign-born residents to the cultural and economic fabric of Atlanta are irrefutable. In the city of Atlanta, immigrants are over-represented among the self-employed, and across our state, new immigrant business owners generate business revenue of $2.9 billion a year" (source: *USCIS Daily Digest Bulletin* – Friday, April 24, 2015).

Before traveling from your country to another country, you will need a traveling visa or authorization document permitting you to enter the new country. The visa is obtained from the embassy of the country you intend to visit. Basically, there are two types of visa: immigrant visa and nonimmigrant visa. The immigrant visa allows the holder to live and work permanently in the country. The nonimmigrant visa is granted to people who want to enter the country temporarily for a specific reason, such as studies, medical care, entertainment, business, vacation, or temporary work. This type of visa usually has a time limitation. With the expiration of the time, the presence of the holder in the country becomes illegal; therefore, that person is then considered an illegal alien or illegal immigrant.

American Diversity Visa Lottery

The US Government, by law, gives out fifty thousand diversity visas (green cards) each year through the Diversity Immigrant Visa Lottery (also known as the Green Card Lottery, US Visa Lottery, or US Immigration Lottery). The US visas offered through the visa lottery grant permanent residence and work status to successful participants. The congressionally mandated Diversity Immigrant Visa Program is administered on an annual basis by the State Department and conducted based on US law, specifically Section 203(c) of the Immigration and Nationality Act (INA).

This law provides for a class of immigrants known as diversity immigrants, "with visas made available to persons from countries with historically low rates of immigration to the United States."

The annual DV program makes 50,000 visas available to persons meeting simple but strict, eligibility requirements.

A computer-generated, random drawing chooses selectees for DVs. The visas are distributed among six geographic regions, and within each region, no single country may receive more than seven percent of the available DVs in any one year. Visas are allocated to nationals of countries with historically lower rates of US immigration. Nationals of countries who have sent more than 50,000 immigrants to the United States over the past five years are not eligible to apply for the Diversity Visa program.

The Department of State implemented the electronic registration system beginning with DV-2005 in order to make the DV process more efficient and secure. The Department utilizes special technology and other means to identify those who commit fraud for the purposes of illegal immigration or those who submit multiple entries. Almost everyone qualifies to participate in the US Green Card Lottery. Applicants must satisfy minimum nationality and education or work experience requirements. There are no age limitations and you can register for the Green Card Lottery if you are living in the United States or in a foreign country.

(source: US State Department website)

Adventurism

With my experience as a deportee from Nigeria, a neighboring country of Ghana, on two separate occasions, I know how it feels to be an illegal alien. One is likely to meet some people who will exhibit attitudes of xenophobia. With the notion that migrating to a richer country will likely change the lifestyle of some people, various adventurous methods are employed by some people to get to richer countries, usually through unorthodox means, especially by nationals of some poorer countries sharing a border with a richer country.

A recent report by the *New York Times* on April 4, 2015, stated in part, that "European leaders were confronted on Monday with humanitarian crisis in the Mediterranean, as estimates as 900 migrants may have died off the Libyan coast this weekend from Bangladesh and Afghanistan in Asia, Syria and Iraq in the Middle East; and African nations such as Gambia, Somalia, Mali, Eritrea, Ghana, Nigeria, Tunisia, Egypt and other developing countries."

This is a manifestation of the fact that people keep fleeing from their countries as a result of poverty, persecution, famine, conflicts, and war to places they can have peace, freedom, and the pursuit of wealth, in spite of the risks involved in such adventures.

In another development, a press release from US Custom and Border Protection (CBP) dated October 16, 2014, states, "Border Patrol Agents apprehended 32 undocumented Haitians, 25 males and 7 females from the treacherous Monito Island. 'Smugglers take advantage of the ignorance and vulnerability of migrants to leave them stranded in the unihabited Island,' said Ramilo Carrilo, Chief Patrol Agent for the CBP Ramey Border Sector."

In a similar issue, Immigration and Custom Enforcement (ICE) of the Department of Homeland Security (DHS) is responsible for enforcing the nation's immigration laws and ensuring the departure of removable aliens from the United States. Its agency, Enforcement and Removal Operations, uses its immigration Enforcement Agents (EAs) to identify, arrest, and remove aliens who violate US immigration laws. They are also responsible for the transportation and detention of aliens in ICE custody. ICE operates detention centers throughout the United States that detain illegal aliens who are apprehended and placed in removal proceedings. About 31,000 aliens are held in immigration detentions, including children, in any given day in more than two hundred detention centers, jails, and prisons nationwide. (source: Anil Kalhan, 2010. "Rethinking Immigration Detention" *Columbia Law Review*)

As a beneficiary of the American Diversity Visa Lottery, I entered the United States as a permanent resident, along with my wife and two children, in 1999. I later petitioned for my remaining children. With my permanent resident status, my family and I were permitted to work in the United States. However, the plight of some illegal immigrants can become bizarre because of the intense fear of repatriation either from their homes or workplaces. Some of them leave for their home countries voluntarily never to return, because returning would be a difficult process, if not impossible. Some people also decide to leave voluntarily, especially when they are served with notice by the immigration authorities. Others remain adamant, hoping for a better day of amnesty.

It can be difficult for illegal immigrants to find employment, and those who are lucky to find something may work under unpleasant conditions. In order for some illegal immigrants to regularize their stay in the foreign land, they contract a marriage with a citizen and eventually acquire permanent residence leading to citizenship. In some instances, some of these marriages of convenience end up having difficulties.

Immigration is a very big issue for the developed world,

especially in the United States where I live. The Department of Homeland Security newsletter from November 2014 states, "President Obama will be using executive orders to launch a broad overhaul of the U.S. immigration enforcement system. One of the immediate results would be to shield up to five million undocumented immigrants – nearly half of the estimated 11.5 million undocumented immigrants currently in the United States – from threat of deportation."

Most illegal immigrants in the United States are Hispanics, and many cross the Mexican border into the US Southwest. California has the highest number of illegal immigrants (estimated at 2.4 million in 2012) but has not seen that population grow as quickly as many other states, including Florida, Illinois, New Jersey, New York, and Texas. (source: Reuters/Pew Research Analysis of November 18, 2014)

Some immigrants enter the United States on student visas and are expected to return to their home countries but fail to go back, thus becoming illegal aliens. As a matter of fact, some of these students aspiring for their master's and other degrees experience such untold financial hardships in the course of the academic pursuits that they eventually abandon their studies and look for work. According to Homeland Security News of September 9, 2014, "The Department of Homeland Security (DHS) has lost tabs on more than 6,000 foreign students who had entered the United States on student visas which have expired – effectively vanishing without trace. According to Senator Tom Coburn, (R-Oklahoma), 'they get the visas and they disappear.'"

Notwithstanding their plight, some illegal immigrants indulge in some nefarious activities in their host countries. Immigration authorities in Ghana state that "more than 4,500 Chinese nationals have been repatriated after a series of swoops on illegal gold miners. The Chinese have attracted heavy criticism from Ghanaians for taking local jobs, wielding weapons such as A.K – 47 rifles and polluting lakes and rivers" (source: Daily Graphic Online.com).

In the United States and other developed countries, some illegal aliens have been arrested for various criminal activities, including murder, drug trafficking, assault, human trafficking, and money laundering, and have been sentenced to various prison sentences or deported.

Immigrant Organizations

In view of the diversity of immigrant communities in Chicago and the United States as a whole, various immigrant organizations have come together to form a bigger organization known as the Illinois Coalition for Immigrant and Refugee Rights (ICIRR). The membership of this coalition includes the following organizations: Hispanic American Community Education and Services, United African Organization, Polish American Association, Vietnamese Association of Illinois, Hebrew Immigrant Aid Society, Indo-American Center, Chinese Mutual Aid Association, Alliance of Filipinos for Immigrant Rights and Empowerment, Arab American Action Network, Assyrian National Council of Illinois, Cambodia Association of Illinois, Chicago Irish Immigrant Support, Ethiopian Community Association of Chicago, Iraqi Mutual Aid Society, Dominican Literary Center–Aurora, Council on American-Islamic Relations, and Asian American Action Network.

The ICIRR is dedicated to promoting the rights of immigrants and refugees to full and equal participation in civic, cultural, social, and political life of this diverse society. In partnership with more than 130 member organizations, ICIRR educates and organizes immigrant and refugee communities to assert their rights; promotes citizenship and civic participation; monitors, analyzes, and advocates on immigrant-related issues; and informs the general public about the contributions of immigrants and refugees.

On a related note, the United African Organization (UAO), a relatively new group under the leadership of its executive director, Dr. Alie Kabba, is working assiduously to put the organization on equal footing with the other established groups. He is assisted by Ms. Nancy Asirifi-Otchere, the organization's program coordinator. UAO is a dynamic coalition of African community-based organizations that promotes social and economic justice, civic participation, and empowerment of African immigrants and refugees in Illinois. It also engages in activities that promote the cultural, educational, social, and economic empowerment of African immigrants and refugees. The UAO also provides assistance with immigration issues. Furthermore, it provides leadership and organizational capacity training for African community-based organizations through the Community Leadership Program. It also facilitates access to community development resources and employment opportunities.

APPENDIX 4

ASANTEMAN ASSOCIATION OF CHICAGO AND MIDWEST

Brief History

The Asanteman Association consists of people from Asanteman, one of the ethnic groups from the major Akan tribe of Ghana. The Asantes (corrupted name Ashanti) people owe absolute allegiance to the Asantehene, the supreme head of the people. The capital city is Kumasi.

The Asanteman Association of Chicago and Midwest had a very modest beginning in the late 1970s on the south side of Chicago. It was the third such association of Asantefuo in North America, after New York in the United States and Toronto in Canada. The pillar behind the formation of the association was Wofa (Uncle) Kojo Renner, who voluntarily offered his house as the meeting place for the infant association. He was selected by the members as the interim chairman to oversee the affairs of the group.

Following is a list of some of the leading members of the association during its formative years: Nana Alex Prempeh, Nana Wiafe-Bonsu, Barima Osei Abebrese, Nana Atakora

Amaniampong Messrs Akwasi Mensah Sarpong, Adu Darkwah, and Victor Owusu. The new association elected Mr. Adu Darkwah as the chairman and Nana Serwaa Akoto as Asantefuohemaa (queen). Nana Atakora Amaniampong succeeded Mr. Adu Darkwah, while Nana Adwoa Pinamang succeeded Nana Serwaa Akoto as chairman and queen respectively. Nana Atakora Amaniampong instituted the chieftaincy and thereby became the first Asantefuohene (chief of Asantefuo). The next chief was Nana Wiafe Bonsu with Nana Yaa Pokuah as the Asantefuohemaa, but during his second term, Nana Akua Takyiwaa became the queen.

There was a formal inauguration to coronate Nana Wiafe Bonsu as the traditionally installed Asantefuohene. He was very instrumental in the formation of the Asanteman Council of North America (ACONA), which is the umbrella organization of all Asante Associations of North America, including those in the United States and Canada. However, Nana Wiafe Bonsu stepped down during the first year of his second term of leadership, and Nana Akwasi Appiah was selected to complete the remaining years of that term. He was later elected as the Asantefuohene of Chicago, and Nana Amma Akyaa served as the Asantefuohemaa of Chicago and the Midwest. They served for two terms of three years each. A formal inauguration was organized for their coronation. Nana Akwasi Appiah continued to build on the good works of his predecessors. He led a delegation of Asanteman Association of Chicago to participate in a grand convention in honor of Otumfour (Majesty) Osei Tutu II, the Asantehene at Pontiac, Detroit. (source: Asantemanchicago.org)

The Asanteman Association of Chicago and Midwest, at a general meeting on Sunday, October 27, elected Opanin Akwasi Addae as the new Asantefuohene and Nana Abena Amponsah as the Asantefuohemaa. Nana Akwasi Addae succeeded Nana Akwasi Appiah, while Nana Abena Amponsah succeeded Nana

Amma Akyaah. Nana Akwasi Addae had Nana Yaw Asamoah as his Kontihene (deputy chief) and Nana Addae Baffour as the Akwamuhene, and Nana Abena Amponsah had Nana Akosua Pomaa as Kontihemaa (deputy queen). Nana Akwasi Addai appointed me as his secretary and, for that matter, as the secretary of the association. He further appointed Nana Yaw Sarfo as the Sanaahene (chief of the treasury). He also appointed Nana Kwame Boakye-Yiadom as his Abusua Panin (counselor) and Nana Amofa Brempong-Kwabia as his Okyeame (linguist). Other subchiefs included Nana Kwaku Sarpong, Nana Kofi Oduro, and Nana Yaw Mensah.

On Saturday, May, 23, 2003, my wife and I joined the family of Nana Akwasi Addae and drove to New York City to attend the installation ceremony of Nana Anane Amponsah, the newly installed Asantefuohene of New York and New Jersey. We returned the following Sunday. We traveled a distance of more than eight hundred miles, and it took us about fourteen hours to make the journey each way, to and from New York. Nana Akwasi Addae organized a black tie dinner and dance to raise funds for the association.

It is worthy to note that during Nana Akwasi Addae's leadership, Nana Bennett Barnie Agyeman offered the basement of his house for the association to organize its monthly meetings and other social functions.

At a general meeting of Asanteman Association of Metropolitan Chicago and Midwest held on Sunday, November 26, 2006, members of the association elected Jerry Addae Baffour as the new Asantefuohene of Chicago, and Nana Abena Amponsah retained her position as the Asantefuohemaa of Chicago. Nana Addai Baffour appointed Victor Sakyi Ntow Boafo as the secretary to the Asanteman Association. He still remains the secretary, while I assist him in recording minutes of general meetings. Mrs. Abena Agyeman Bugyei serves as the Youth Coordinator.

The coronation of Nana Addae Baffour and Nana Abena Amponsah as chief and queen, respectively, commenced on May 24, 2008, and ended the next day. It was supervised by Nana Adusei Atenewa Ampem I, who deputized for His Royal Highness Otumfuo Osei Tutu II, the Asantehene. Nana Addae Baffour took the oath of allegiance before Otumfuo's representative. Others who took the oath of allegiance on that great occasion were Nana Yaw Osei Asamoah (John Osei) as Kontihene (deputy chief) and Nana Yaw Sarfo (Seth Owusu) as Sanaahene (chief of the treasury).

Other subchiefs were Nana Kwaku Oduro (Okyeame/ linguist), Nana Yaw Mensah (Akwamuhene), Nana Kwabena Osei (Gyaasehene), Nana Owusu Korkor (Nifahene), Nana Kofi Oduro (Nkosuohene), Nana Kwaku Sarpong (Adontenhene), Nana Akwasi Mensah Abankwa (Mmrantiehene), Nana Sebeh Kwarteng (Manwerehene), Nana Kwabena Agyenim Boateng (Kyidomhene), Nana Kwabena Afriyie (Benkumhene), Nana Kwame Frimpong (Akyempemhene), Nana Akwasi Agyekum (Nsumankwaahene), and Nana Yaw Opoku (Ankobeahene). All swore allegiance to the Nana Adusei Atenewa Ampem I. On the women's side were Nana Akosua Pomaa as Kontihemaa (deputy queen) and Nana Afua Drowaa (Akwamuhemaa). The members of the Council of Elders (Abusua Mpaninfuo) were Nana Aboagye Manu, Nana Kwaku Duah, Nana Kwasi Antwi Bosiako, and the late Nana Kofi Anning. Others were Mrs. Sally Owusu, Mrs. Betty Agyeman, and Nana Akosua Afriyie. It is the job of the Council of Elders to counsel and guide the chief, the queen, and all the subchiefs. They also arbitrate and mediate in case of any disputes between members of the association.

This memorable ceremony attracted delegations from the Asanteman Associations of New York City; Denver; Washington, DC; Atlanta; Texas; and Toronto, Canada, led by their chiefs and queens to give moral support to their sister association.

A delegation from the Asanteman Council of North America (ACONA) was in attendance.

The traditional leaders of the various associations in Chicago were in attendance as well. They included Nana Yaw Adu Gyamfi and Nana Abena Pokuah of the Brong-Ahafo Association, Nana Kwabena Koranteng and Nana Efuah Anamuah I of Fanti Benevolent Society, Mantse Nii Armah Akonfrah I and Manye Naa Dedei Amobiye I of GaDangme Community Organization, and Alhaji Sulemana Giwa and Magajia Sekina Mohammed of the Haske Society. Also in attendance were Nana Kwame Asamoah and Ohemaa Akosua Asantewaa of Kwahu United Association, Naa Issah Samori and Pagnaa Hajia Habiba Fuseini of the Ghana Northern Union, Nana Yirenkyi Bonsu I and Ohemaa Akosua Pokuah of Okuapeman Fekuo, Nana Akwafo Adu Brempong II and Ohemaa Akua Owusuaa of Okyeman Association, and the late Togbui Venya I and Mama Afua Abeli of Ewe Association. Until his untimely death on May 11, 2014, Togbui Venya I was the president of the Chieftaincy Council of Chicago. He has since been replaced by Togbui Simon Addo. The Chairman of the Ghana Chicago Club, A.C Eddie-Quartey, and the chairman of the GaDangme Community Organization, Abdul Brimah, also attended. The presidents of the various associations, including Joe Konadu of Brong-Ahafo Association, Dr. Mark Kutame of Ewe Association, Rev. Emmanuel Amonoo of Fanti Benevolent Society, Alfa Tanim Mohammed of the Haske Society, John Kesse of Kwahu United Association, Eddie Anoba of Okuapeman Fekuo, and Dr. Joseph Ankomah of Ghana Northern Union, were all present at the ceremony. All important Ghanaian personalities were also in attendance to grace the occasion. (source: 2008 GhanaFest brochure)

The former Asantefuohene of Chicago, Nana Akwasi Appiah and Nana Akwasi Addae, were also in attendance. Nana Baffour

Antwi Gyeabuor, a traditional leader, some founding members of Asanteman in the persons of Osei Abebrese, Kojo Renner, Atakora Amaniampong were also in attendance. The masters of ceremonies were Nana Wiafe Akenteng, Nana Bosomprah Ampem, and Mr. Essah Mensah, who was then the public relations officer of ACONA. Incidentally, Essah Mensah was my classmate and roommate at T.I. AMASS. This memorable event took place at the Grand Ballroom at Sixty-Third Street and Cottage Grove Avenue on the south side of Chicago.

REFERENCES

As much as I relied heavily on my personal journal, memory, and oral history, I did consult a lot of periodicals, newspapers, *African Spectrum* newspaper, Ghana Web, and other websites, as well as some books, some of which are worth mentioning.

Adams; Leah D., and Anna Kirova. *Global Migration and Education*. New Jersey: Lawrence Erlbaum Associates Inc., 2006.

Baker Kline, Christina. *Orphan Train*. New York: Harper Collins, 2013.

Comer, James P., and Charlayne Hunter-Gault. *Maggie's American Dream: The Life and Times of a Black Family*. New York: Penguin Books USA, 1989.

Dicks, Matthew. *Memoirs of an Imaginary Friend*. New York: St. Martin's Press, 2012.

Effah, Benjamin Adu Kwadwo. *The Secrets of Marital Success*. Accra, Ghana: Unique Xpressions, 2010.

Laye, Camara. *The African Child*. Glasgow, Great Britain: Fontana Books, 1959.

Mbiti, John S. *African Religions and Philosophy, Second Edition*. Norfolk: Great Britain, Biddles Ltd, King's Lynn.

Nichols, Lisa. *No Matter What: 9 Steps to Living the Life You Love.* New York: Hachette Book Group, 2009.

Obama, Barack. *Dreams from My Father: A Story of Race and Inheritance.* New York: Three Rivers Press, 2004.

Robbins, Richard H. *Cultural Anthropology: A Problem-Based Approach.* Belmont, California: Wadsworth, Cengage, 2009.

Solomon, Jeremy. *Newcomers Handbook for Moving to and Living in Chicago.* Portland, OR: First Books, 2004.

Printed in the United States
By Bookmasters